12 things I learned at 18 !!!

1. Yesterday is history, tomorrow is a mystery, and today is a gift—that's why it's called the present.

2. Work for your own dreams, or someone else will hire you to build theirs.

3. If your 'why' is strong, there will be no excuses for resting.

4. Patience is key.

5. Consistency is the key to success.

6. Smart work in the right direction matters more than just hard work.

7. Books are your best friends—they hold the knowledge of the world.

8. Be your best every day to become the best version of yourself.

9. Problems are not obstacles; they are steps toward success.

10. Your network is your net worth

11. Growth comes from discomfort.

12. Success is a journey, not a destination—have commas, but no full stops.

Chapter 1

Yesterday is history, tomorrow is a mystery, and today is a gift—that's why it's called the present

In a world that whirls at breakneck speed, it's much too simple to become ensnared in the cycle of past regrets or anxiety about future concerns. We often find ourselves ruminating over choices we've made in the past, wishing we could turn back the clock, or we become bogged down in anxiety about the future, fretting over things that have no possibility of ever occurring. But the reality is, the only moment we can truly claim as our own is the present— this very moment we are experiencing now.

This chapter delves into the value of living in the present, showing that it is not merely a comforting notion but a crucial success strategy for our work and life. By releasing the grip of fixed past occurrences and putting our energy toward what we can accomplish today, we empower ourselves to create our future in a positive manner. Becoming master of this concept can transform our thinking, allowing us to construct a more fulfilling and productive life.

Embracing the Past: Making Experience Strength Every individual has had a past full of things he or she would rather not recall. It may be a school failure, job loss, or the end of a significant relationship. These incidents may burden us if allowed. However, the past should be regarded as a rearview mirror—a sight to glance at from time to time, but not a factor that diverts our attention from what lies ahead.

Personal Reflection: I had previously devoted hours and a lot of passion to a business venture that ultimately collapsed. A mix of naivety and some bad decisions caused it to fail, regardless of my effort. I stayed in a cycle of self-doubt for a long period, always questioning my decisions: What if I had done differently? Why didn't I see those obstacles coming? This ongoing reflection on my past drained my motivation and self-esteem.

Inspirational Conclusion: Ultimately, I came to a deep realization: that failure was not the end of my tale, but rather a chapter in it. The things I learned from the experience were priceless. They provided me with a sense of resiliency, improved my risk management skills, and, most importantly, taught me that failure is not the end unless I make it that way. The most valuable lesson is that past blunders are not to be considered obstacles to advancement; rather, they are to be utilized as excellent guides to future triumph. Your past need not imprison you; rather, it should shape and enrich your growth.

The future is unpredictable, with twists and turns that can take anyone by surprise. No matter how much we plan or prepare, life itself has a way of surprising us with unplanned events. This uncertainty is not to be feared but a fertile soil for development, both personally and professionally. In the space of uncertainty lies a treasure chest of possibilities waiting to be explored, and the acceptance of this uncertainty can be the source of stunning transmutations.

Consider the paths of great entrepreneurs such as Steve Jobs and Elon Musk. Theirs were far from being linear routes, riddled with colossal setbacks and failures. Jobs envisioned himself being ousted from the company he founded, whereas Musk envisioned a number of roadblocks for SpaceX before he could Savor success. Nevertheless, the two persevered, oblivious to the uncertainty that was yet to dawn on them. They knew that dwelling on the likelihood of future challenges would not shield them from them; instead, they opted to take proactive steps in the present.

If you are struggling with uncertainty—whether it is the fate of your business, discovering your purposeful vocation, or the path of your life—remember that excessive concern can drain the energy and focus from you. Instead of worrying about the future, place your attention on the areas of your life over which you can exert effort in the present day. The humble, conscious actions you take today can create the potential tomorrow has to offer. Embrace the future as an intriguing journey, and while preparation is necessary, don't allow fear of the unknown to stall your advancement.

The significance of the moment cannot be overstated; it is a truism that "the best time to have started was yesterday, but the second best time is now." It is not motivational jargon; it is a firm reminder that action is needed. Being in the moment allows us to take hold of opportunities that have the potential to bring profound change into our lives.

Think about the idea of the Compound Effect, which shows how small, consistent steps day after day can accumulate to create incredible results. Just as compound interest is formed in the financial sector, the effects of our work will not always be seen, but through persistent effort, they will manifest in deep ways. This is the invitation to take that initial step, however insignificant it might be, because it has the potential to create revolutionary results.

If I look at my own life, I used to believe that initiating change for the better was a task of Herculean size. But I discovered that real success is a question of a series of small, daily routines. For instance, dedicating just 20 minutes a day to reading might not be of much significance in the beginning, but over the period of a year, it can lead to the reading of more than 15 books, each one of which enhances my knowledge and alters my perspective. Imagine what can happen if you devoted some portion of the day to personal development, skill acquisition, or business pursuits; success may perhaps not be instant, but it is certain to be so, day by day.

Being present actually makes you have more fun and enjoy life. One of the greatest things you can do to start your day is to have a clear intention. Take one minute in the morning and think about a specific activity that can propel you toward your goal. It can be something as mundane as making a phone call, doing a small task, or doing a hobby. By concentrating on this one task, you create a sense of purpose that will propel your day and keep you going, even with distractions.

Having gratitude in your daily life can also shift your thinking. Try to take a few moments each day to write down three things that you are thankful for in your life. It appears to make your thinking shift from what you do not have to what is already present in your life. Another aspect is taking time to be present. Whatever it is, smelling the scent of your coffee in the morning or taking in nature with a walk, be sure you stay present to what you are sensing. If your mind gets caught up again in regrets of the past or worries of the future, gently take your mind back to the here and now and take deliberate action toward what you can control here and now.

Looking at our lives, we realize that while the past is rich in lessons and the future is rich in promise, it is the present that actually makes our lives. Today is the only moment we have to create our own experiences and decisions. Rather than allowing concern about the past that can't be altered or the future that is uncertain to fill your mind, use the gift that today provides. Live intentionally in your world, take positive action towards your dreams, and Appreciate the moments that slip away.

It is important to understand the importance of the moment. Yesterday is the past, and it is something that can be learned from, and tomorrow's uncertainties do not have to make you afraid but curious. Use today as a valuable gift, an opportunity to make memories and learn. Make sure that you live every moment, for it is in this very day that you can actually live, flourish, and enjoy the journey that lies ahead.

Reflection Questions for the Reader:

1. What's one lesson from your past that you can use to grow today?
2. What small step can you take right now to move closer to your goals?
3. Are you living in the moment, or are you stuck in the past or future?

Chapter 2

Work for your own dreams, or someone else will hire you to build theirs

Picture waking up every morning, not because you want to, but because you have to. You clock in and out, trapped in a daily routine, your passion not on your dreams but on living for someone else. This is the daily grind for so many, but it doesn't have to be yours.

This chapter challenges you to take hold of your own life and retake the power that is rightfully yours. This reiterates the value of investing in your own desires and aspirations; else you will pass your entire lifetime building someone else's dream. It is up to you: are you to be a player of your own destiny, or a spectator of someone else's game?

The Price of Not Pursuing Your Dreams Not pursuing your dreams has a very high price tag that is not only financial, but also emotional, mental, and spiritual. The danger is that you will live a life of regret, frustration, and constant barrage of "what ifs" in your head. The abandonment can produce an emptiness that permeates all aspects of your life, and you feel that you yearn for something more meaningful.

Personal Experience: I had a period in my life where I worked only for the pay check that it brought. The job was stable and had a wonderful work environment, but every day was a chore. I counted down the hours until the weekends, waiting for the day when I could leave the drudgery of my daily routine behind. The real problem wasn't the job; it was that I had put my real passions and dreams on the backburner, letting them collect dust in the corners of my mind.

A Critical Epiphany: I finally came to understand that I was giving away my precious time for money but not for any sense of achievement or joy. This came as a wake-up call and led me to spend my leisure time on my own creative pursuits. Although the process was cumbersome and the development was gradual in the beginning, the thrill, enthusiasm, and meaning I derived made the efforts all the more rewarding. It dawned on me that although a steady pay check may be reassuring, the same reassurance can stifle personal growth and lead to a life spent helping others achieve their dreams instead of yours.

The concept of pursuing one's dreams is typically met with the simple advice to "follow your dreams." But the truth is that most individuals are too afraid to take the leap of faith. The number one reason for this is the pervasive fear. Humans deal with a myriad of fears that can paralyze their dreams, including fear of failure, which appears in the guise of fear of doing something new and being let down. Second, fear of judgment plays a role as well, in the sense that humans fear how others will perceive them when they fail. Lastly, fear of the unknown can be paralyzing, particularly when it comes to securing finances and the unknowns that accompany pursuing a passion.

It must be remembered that failure is not an end but a stepping stone to success. Every great person who has reached great heights has experienced failures in their professional life. The only difference is that they have the courage to face and overcome those fears instead of allowing them to influence their decisions. Take, for example, the case of J.K. Rowling, the great author of the

Harry Potter series. Prior to her giant success, she was rejected by twelve publishers. Each rejection could have easily discouraged her, but she did not give up. She went on to pen a literary phenomenon that has captivated millions of people all over the world.

The moral here is simple: though fear is an innate human sentiment, it shouldn't be in charge of your choices and desires. The acceptance of the fear of failure can open the way to amazing prospects and development. The biggest gamble one can ever make is to never make a gamble, since this will cause one to spend a life regretting and wasting one's own potential. With the acknowledgment and facing of one's fears, and enduring the pain, one can access the full potential within oneself and proceed to the path of actualizing one's goals.

Making dreams a reality requires more than daydreaming; it requires a game plan. What differentiates dreamers from doers is the capability of putting their plan into action. To start down the road of making your dreams a reality without giving up your present commitments, you need to start with a vision of what you truly desire. What is that one thing or one dream that has been in your heart—entrepreneurship, writing a book, visiting other cultures, or pursuing another dream?.

Once you have your dream, the second thing is to divide it into steps which are achievable. Big goals can sometimes be daunting, but by dividing them into steps which are tangible and achievable, you have a direction. If, for instance, your dream is to start a business, your first step can be researching your target market thoroughly or building a simple website to stake your claim on the web. This not only makes the journey less daunting but also means you get to celebrate small victories along the way, and your motivational levels do not hit rock bottom.

Consistency is the secret to this endeavour, so you have to make time every day to work on your dream without necessarily quitting your job or responsibilities. Spending time for only 30 minutes to an hour a day can amount to a lot of progress in the long run. Having a positive group of people around you can also go a long way in your journey. Find people who believe in your vision, whether through community groups, networking groups, or social media. The people you are around can play a big role in your attitude and motivation, turning your dream into a reality.

Embracing the Self-Employment Experience When you embark on the path of chasing your dreams, you're not merely creating a business or reaching a milestone; you're cultivating a sense of autonomy. That autonomy allows you to chart your own course, selecting the path that resonates with your vision. You're free to work on projects that thrill you, and you're free to fail and learn from your mistakes, using those mistakes to add complexity to the richness of your experience.

Personal Reflections regarding the Self-Employment Process My own experience of self-employment has been an emotional rollercoaster ride with setbacks and triumphs. There have been moments when I questioned myself, moments when the challenges that lay between me and success appeared insurmountable, and moments when the urge to call it quits was irresistible. But the exhilarating freedom of waking up each morning knowing that I am building my own destiny—rather than assisting someone else's dream to come true—is worth any hardship. The unique energy and feeling of pride that results from knowing my sweat, blood, and long hours are all being put into a cause that I believe in is quite unbeatable.

The Spirit of Being Your Own Boss At the end of the day, the spirit of being your own boss is not about the money; it's about living a life that is true to your values and your dreams. This endeavour is not about profit; it's about creating a legacy that is a reflection of who you are and what you believe in. The fulfilment that you get from this endeavour is deep, as you are able to take pride in the life that you are creating, one that is true to your dreams and aspirations.

Venturing out to follow your dreams is exhilarating and scary. The first thing you need to do is to have definite and concrete goals. Instead of having vague dreams, specify what you want to achieve. For instance, instead of saying, "I want to venture into a business," specify your goal by stating, "I plan to venture into an online store selling eco-friendly products by this year." Being specific not only provides you with direction but it also serves as a motivational anchor as you proceed.

Another excellent strategy is to create a vision board that captures your dreams and wishes. The visual board may include pictures, inspirational quotes, and symbols that represent your dreams. Having these reminders in front of you gives you a sense of motivation and focus that can propel you to take action. The act of visualizing yourself succeeding can reinforce your determination and remind you of your goals so that it becomes second nature to stay focused.

Lastly, investing in personal development is crucial to your success. Read books, take courses, and learn from people who have successfully done the path you wish to take. Knowledge is a precious resource that can guide you in making the right decisions. Risk-taking is also involved in the process, but do it cautiously. You don't need to leave your current job right away; instead, start gradually, step by step, that builds your confidence and momentum so that you can make the seamless transition when the time is right.

The last decision is yours. You can pursue your own wishes, though one fraught with issues, doubt, and forty years of toil. Or, you can assist another person in realizing his dreams, trading your valuable hours for a pay check but losing the satisfaction of realizing your own dreams. This brings about a very pertinent question: what kind of life would you want to wake up to each morning?

Taking the road to your dreams is always an alternative, wherever you are today. The initial step is daunting, but it is also the most liberating choice you will ever take. The future belongs to you for those who dare to dream and are strong enough to chase those dreams with Vigor. Take the road forward, for it is littered with opportunities waiting to be seized.

Reflection Questions for the Reader:

1. What's one dream you've put on hold, and why?
2. What's one small step you can take today to start working towards your dream?
3. Are you living a life that excites you, or are you building someone else's vision?

Chapter 3

If your 'why' is strong, there will be no excuses for resting

Did you ever stop to think why some individuals can Plow through tough times and emerge stronger on the other end, whereas others break at the first obstacle? The secret to this resilience is encapsulated in one word: purpose. Your purpose is the underlying reason for what you do, a wellspring of energy that drives you forward, particularly in tough times. When you do not have a clear purpose, it is all too simple to fall prey to excuses, lose heart, or drop aspirations. On the other hand, a clear purpose enables you to Plow through obstacles, whether they are in the form of setbacks, criticism, or plain exhaustion.

This chapter explores the journey of discovering your purpose and incorporating it as the cornerstone of your endeavours. Defining your purpose lights your way, not just making it simpler to walk but also more rewarding. A sense of purpose converts failures into stepping stones so that you can stay firm and unfazed. With a strong purpose, you become unbreakable, ready to face whatever life throws your way with energy and resolve.

Knowing your underlying motivation is crucial to living a meaningful life. Your motivation goes beyond ambitions like getting a pay check or reaching the top of the corporate ladder; it reaches into the very core of what drives your soul. This intrinsic motivation is what gets you up every morning, even when exhaustion presses upon you. It is your beacon in times of turmoil, offering the strength required to weather the uncertainty of life.

Powerful motivations usually represent intense desires that deeply resonate with us. For example, some individuals may harbour a strong motivation to improve the lives of their family, whereas others might feel driven to prove themselves and attain personal greatness. There are individuals who are content with inspiring others by imparting their knowledge and experience, and there are others who are motivated by the desire to make an enduring impact that makes the world a better place. These reasons are not mere passing thoughts; they are strong motivations that determine our actions and choices.

Looking back at my own experience, I had initially thought that my main drive was to achieve financial freedom. But as I faced different challenges, it became apparent that money alone could not fuel my motivation. The real nature of my drive was a need for freedom—the freedom to be myself, provide for my loved ones, and motivate others to follow their own way. After I accepted this higher purpose, I started to see obstacles as opportunities for development, turning failures into lessons learned instead of impossible obstacles.

It's a cliche that excuses are the path of least resistance. Cliched phrases like "I'm too tired," "I'll do it tomorrow," or "I don't have the money or the time" are all too frequent. These excuses will come up when the inner motivation is absent. If your excuse is fuzzy and insignificant, it's too convenient to resort to feelings of tiredness, anxiety, or uncertainty. But if your reason for achieving your goal is clear and substantial, you'll find the energy to overcome barriers that stand in your way.

Consider the lives of legendary athletes such as Michael Jordan and Serena Williams. It is hard to envision them ever feeling fatigued or demotivated. And yet, their persistent drive—a flame that would never be doused until they were the best, set new records, and inspired millions—was so strong that they never thought of giving up. Their commitment to their "why" carried them through the darkest moments, demonstrating that a great purpose can be a great motivator.

The key to remember here is that if your motivation level is high, excuses can never stand the test. A clear purpose serves like a bulletproof vest against the allure of laziness and doubt. By grounding yourself in a good reason for what you're doing, you set a foundation to enable you to overcome obstacles and stand firm on your journey. Essentially, a good "why" turns obstacles into stepping stones to success.

Finding your life purpose is not an easy path, sometimes necessitating a plunge into the very depths of your own thoughts and emotions. It is something that involves looking within and facing your real self. But when you find this deeper reason for being, it becomes a beacon of light that illuminates the complexities of life with purpose and will.

To start this process, start by questioning yourself with questions of importance. Question yourself what truly excites you and what you are drawn to naturally, even without the possibility of financial reward. Question yourself who or whom you need to empower or motivate. These are important questions because they set the stage for understanding what truly is most important to you and what you wish to achieve.

As you delve deeper into your motivations, keep in mind that the first answers may be merely scratching the surface. Challenge yourself by asking yourself "Why?" repeatedly and stripping away the layers of your desires. For example, if your desire is to be an entrepreneur, delve deeper into why you wish to be one. Is it not only for the money, but also freedom and the power to provide for your loved ones as well? This deeper understanding of your motivations can be a rich reservoir of resilience, motivating you even when the going gets rough.

Life is simply full of challenges and adversity that tend to make you want to quit and get frustrated. On those really bad days, when you don't want to do anything and you question everything, it is your underlying purpose that is a strong anchor. This underlying motivation behind your actions is the lifeline that you hold on to when the world around you seems to be in disarray and out of control.

Consider the example of starting a new business venture. In the early months, you may be experiencing meagre sales and frustration. If success in terms of money is the only driving force, the temptation to quit will become overwhelming. But if you are motivated by a desire to ensure a brighter future for your family members or to help others fulfil their dreams, you are very likely to overcome the hump and hold on to your dream.

You need to shift your attitude towards the challenges you're facing. Rather than viewing these challenges as insurmountable barriers that you should conquer, view them as challenges that are worth testing your will and determination. Each challenge is a chance to reaffirm your commitment to your cause, and by doing so, you become tougher and more resilient in the quest for your goals.

The connection between your passion and your purpose runs deep. If you are engaged in activities that you love, the process itself is a delight, not one to be gotten through. Challenges will arise, certainly, but the passion for what you're doing is a powerful motivator to keep pushing forward even with adversity.

One of the greatest examples of this dynamic is the life of Elon Musk. His business ventures, such as SpaceX and Tesla, were not merely about profit; they were about a grander purpose of making the future of humanity better. Whether it is through the development of sustainable energy technologies or the ambitious goal of establishing a human colony on Mars, Musk's laser-like focus powers his work habit, enabling him to work hundreds of hours on his vision, unfazed by failure in the process.

There are countless stories to be told, stories of people who have lived their purpose. Oprah Winfrey's is one of them that is motivated by a passion to inspire and empower others. Born into poverty, having had to struggle through many obstacles in her path, Oprah's tireless commitment to her profession has seen her not only become a media mogul, but a source of inspiration of strength and empowerment to millions of individuals. Her own story is an inspiration to the kind of change that living purposefully and with passion can create.

And still another inspirational life is that of Nelson Mandela, whose abiding enthusiasm for freedom transcended individual desire to include the freedom of his country at large. Imprisoned for 27 years, Mandela never faltered, sustained by a sense of purpose that extended beyond his circumstances. His is a life that speaks to the power of a sense of purpose to carry a human being through the darkest of circumstances. As you look back at your own journey, remember that you are the author of your own book; your own sense of purpose can be equally transformative, in whatever direction you travel.

In order to help your cause, start by stating your primary motivation in brief words. Write it down and place it somewhere you will see it daily, such as on your wall, in your phone, or between the pages of your journal. The reminder will keep you focused and committed to your path, and your "why" will always be at the back of your mind daily.

Second, practice visualization of success. Imagine vividly what your life will be like once you've reached success, becoming one with the emotions of success. Visualization can be a strong motivator, driving you to success. Third, make sure your goals are highly connected to your purpose. Every goal needs to be a stepping stone to achieving your overall mission. Finally, share your purpose with a trusted friend or mentor; having someone to hold you accountable can significantly decrease the desire to make excuses and keep you moving forward.

In life, challenges and setbacks are unavoidable. But when you have a compelling reason for what you do, no challenge will seem insurmountable. This reason is the driving force that is the light that leads you even in the darkest of times. It is the fuel for your will, the energy to push through fatigue and the strength to confront your fears. Your purpose is not a fleeting thought; it is the essence of your journey, the force that propels you forward and turns dreams into tangible realities.

So, spend some time thinking about your own motivations. What is that really driving you? Finding that inner purpose is important, because it will allow you to cut through the obstacles of life with direction and purpose. Take your purpose for yourself entirely, and let it direct you to a successful and fulfilling life. By finding your home in this profound sense of your why, you can create a life of purpose and attainment, skipping over any obstacles that arise in your path.

Reflection Questions for the Reader:

1. What drives me to wake up and work hard every day?
2. When faced with challenges, do I have a strong enough *why* to keep going?
3. How can I align my daily actions with my deeper purpose?

Chapter 4

Patience is key

In today's world, instant gratification is around every corner. We have become accustomed to the convenience of fast food, instant messaging, quick delivery, and swift results. But with the big objectives, we need to realize that actual achievement is not immediate. The greatest satisfaction is obtained by investing long time and effort.

Regardless of what one is doing to create a successful business, learn a new skill, or become a better individual, patience is the virtue that is needed. This chapter talks about the importance of enjoying the process, believing in the process, and understanding that long-term success is not the result of speed but the outcome of unrelenting commitment, persistence, and the transfer of time.

The Myth of Instant Success Each time we hear stories of people who have attained remarkable success, we automatically assume that they had that moment of eureka. But in most cases, the reality is quite different, as the stories usually conceal the numerous hours of determination, failures, and unshakable will that led them to their victory. Success is never linear or easy; it is a tapestry woven with failure and success that characterizes an individual's journey.

Look at the life of famous individuals such as Steve Jobs, who was humiliated by being removed from the company he started, only to come back and build Apple into a worldwide giant. Equally, Colonel Sanders was rejected more than a thousand times before someone was ready to adopt his KFC idea, showcasing the strength needed to turn an idea into reality. J.K. Rowling's tale is no exception; she was a welfare-dependent single mother, struggling with her own issues, before the Harry Potter books made her a literary superstar. These instances show that the path to success is usually filled with hardships that challenge one's determination.

The most important lesson of these stories is that what might seem to be an "overnight success" is really the result of a long and hard road with many lessons learned along the way. Success is not a straight line; it is a circuitous path that requires patience, persistence, and perseverance in the face of adversity. Coming to terms with this fact can help us cherish the hard work of others and motivate us to carry on in our own pursuit, however insurmountable they might be.

The struggle to develop patience is one that most of us can identify with. In a world that lives on instant gratification, waiting can be an uphill climb. We tend to want things right away, and when those results don't come as quickly as we want them to, it can create frustration and even burnout. This restlessness sometimes makes us give up on our objectives too early, only to find ourselves asking what could have been had we just kept waiting a little longer.

There are a number of reasons why we struggle to be patient. One of the key reasons is the tendency to compare ourselves with others. When we see peers making progress at a fast rate, it can plant seeds of self-doubt regarding our own path and process. Moreover, the fear of failure is also present; we might tell ourselves that if we do not get immediate results, it means there is something wrong with our method. This attitude can prove to be counterproductive, as it tends to result in the absence of motivation when we don't witness any immediate progress in our work.

Looking back on my own life, I remember a time when I was impatient for quick returns from my efforts. The early signs of no progress caused me to be downhearted, making me doubt my path and decisions. But with the passage of time, I realized that development is a gradual process, occurring in phases. Those initial setbacks were not symptoms of defeat but rather necessary adjustments that provided the foundation for success down the road. Adopting this mindset has enabled me to develop a greater sense of patience and perseverance in my endeavours.

The process of fulfilling your dreams can be compared to growing a tree from its initial stages. First, you need to plant the seed, which represents the birth of your dreams. This is the phase where you set specific goals, start new ventures, and learn the skills that will propel you in the right direction. It's a time of hope with endless possibilities as you set the stage for the future.

As you move forward, the emphasis is on building the roots, which are the necessary but frequently unseen efforts that support your growth. This stage is marked by late nights spent refining your craft, pushing through challenges, and learning valuable lessons from both triumphs and setbacks. While the fruits of your labour might not be immediately visible, this initial work is essential because it strengthens your capacity to resist adversity and primes you for greater success to come. Eventually, with perseverance and unshakeable dedication, you will arrive at the point of blooming and flourishing. This is when your commitment starts to bear fruit in concrete form, revealing the loveliness of your labour. But let's not forget that without the strong root system, the blooms might not survive. A strong example of this principle can be seen in the bamboo tree growing, as it spends five years cultivating its roots before shooting up a whopping 90-plus feet in six weeks. This extraordinary development bears witness to the resilience acquired in those early years underground.

The Danger of Giving Up Too Soon Too many people give up on their endeavours mere seconds before they reach the point of triumph. They spend a great deal of time and effort, overcoming many barriers in the process, but when instant success eludes them, they opt to quit. Such a situation is all too familiar, as the temptation of immediate reward tends to outweigh the benefit of persistence. Think of the metaphor of digging for gold. Following months of persistent excavation, you're discouraged and tired and think about quitting. What if the treasure you're searching for is literally one swing of the pickaxe away? A great number of individuals don't have any idea how close they are to their moment of triumph and quit, depriving themselves of the fruits of their labour. The moral of this is that persistence is key; you might be nearer to your aspirations than you imagine.

Embracing the Rhythm of Your Journey Life may turn out as we do not plan, but that is just fine. The universe only moves as it will, and what we perceive as a setback is often an opportunity for growth. Instead of seeing delays as challenges, we can appreciate them as important moments for self-improvement, learning, and readying ourselves for opportunities yet to come.

Personal Insight: Looking back, I see that there were times when I was disappointed with the speed of progress. But with hindsight, I know that those times of waiting were important. They enabled me to develop my skills, change my mindset, and develop the resilience to accept the success that finally came.

Creating long-term goals is critical, but also don't forget to acknowledge and celebrate the smaller victories along the way. Those incremental wins are critical signposts of movement, reminding you that each step you take is in the right direction. By noting those markers, not only do you keep yourself motivated but also create a sense of accomplishments that drives you towards your broader objectives. Consistency is the most important thing, particularly in hard times when the drive to get up and try will be lost. It is getting up every day and working despite how you feel that creates the success in the end. It's the small, persistent efforts that pile up over the long term and work better than those occasional frenzied fits of effort. Taking on this attitude will assist you in developing resilience and stay focused, even when the going gets rough.

It is important to avoid comparing your own path to the path of another, as each person's experience is different. Instead, focus on your personal development and achievements. Being grateful for where you are and the progress you've made creates an attitude of patience and satisfaction. Also, if you can see your final objective, it is a great booster that reminds you of your very first inspiration and keeps you energized when faced with adversity.

The life of Thomas Edison is an incredible inspiration to the patient virtue. In his dogged search for the lightbulb, he struggled through over a thousand failed endeavours. Instead of regarding these failure experiences as negatives, Edison's words have inspired many: "I have not failed.". I've just found 1,000 ways that won't work." This perspective not only highlights his resilience but also underscores how his unwavering determination ultimately led to a groundbreaking invention that illuminated the world and transformed daily life.

Walt Disney's success was preceded by a series of difficulties and setbacks that would have demoralized most. First turned down by a newspaper for allegedly having no imagination, he experienced a string of rejections and even threatened bankruptcy. And yet, by sheer determination and an unwavering faith in his dream, Disney ended up creating one of the greatest entertainment dynasties of all time. His is a very poignant reminder that success is rarely smooth sailing and that patience and perseverance can make great things happen.

Looking back at one's own life can uncover the deep influence of patience in one's own life. Think of a time when you were struggling but decided to keep going, even though the odds were against you. Whether it was at work, in school, or in relationships, that determination to push through can bring about incredible outcomes. These kinds of experiences show how patience is not just a waiting game; it is an active involvement in challenges that can ultimately result in positive ends.

Practical Exercises to Develop Patience: First, imagine your goals for the next five years. Spend a moment defining your long-term objectives and then breaking them down into achievable milestones. It's important to understand that realizing major ambitions is a process that takes time, and every small success adds to your overall advancement. Second, think about keeping a journal committed to recording your experiences and progress. This reflective exercise will be a useful tool in times of self-doubt, enabling you to look back at your previous successes and admire the distance you've covered on your path. Finally, challenge yourself with particular tasks that are aimed at building your patience. Take on activities that require persistent effort, like learning a new skill, reading a long book, or working on a difficult project. Remember to enjoy the journey, to celebrate each step of the way instead of just looking forward to the end.

Chapter 5

Consistency is the key to success

Introduction: The Power of Daily Commitment Have you ever wondered what sets those who accomplish their aspirations apart from those who just dream about them? The key is in one simple word: consistency. It has nothing to do with the requirement for perfection, better tools, natural ability, or just chance. The real secret to success lies in the willingness to be there every day no matter what your challenges are or how you are feeling.

Though consistency might be dull in comparison to more exciting characteristics, it is the essential component that turns good efforts into incredible results. Throughout this chapter, we will discuss the importance of consistency, how it creates momentum with the passage of time and finally succumbs to success. We will also explore practical tips to instil this essential habit into your daily life, so you can maximize its power in your pursuit to attain your dreams.

The Importance of Consistency Over Raw Talent It's not uncommon to encounter individuals who possess remarkable talent yet fail to make significant strides in their careers. Conversely, you may also observe those with seemingly average abilities who achieve extraordinary success. The underlying reason for this disparity often lies in the fact that while talent can provide an initial advantage, it is the unwavering commitment to consistent effort that ultimately leads to lasting success.

Consider, for example, the great basketball player Michael Jordan. His natural ability was undeniable, but it was his dogged commitment to practice—perfecting his craft by shooting thousands of shots day after day—that cemented his place as one of the all-time greats. Likewise, think about the path of J.K. Rowling, who didn't create the world of Harry Potter in a single night. Rather, she struggled through many obstacles, writing every day even when in dire financial need, which ultimately culminated into her colossal achievement.

The most important lesson from these illustrations is apparent: although talent is what brings the initial attention, it is the strength of perseverance that pushes individuals ahead in their endeavours. Ongoing effort not only creates competence over a period of time but also gives birth to persistence and resilience, aspects that are most crucial in crossing hurdles and succeeding in the long run. Ultimately, it is the continuous, consistent effort that turns potential into actuality.

The Compound Effect principle teaches that great things are not the product of one grand effort, but the result of small, consistent actions repeated over time. This is similar to saving money; although putting in a little money every day might not seem like much at first, those savings add up and can result in great wealth. In the same way, the efforts we put into our personal and professional lives might seem insignificant in isolation, but when taken together, they can bring about incredible changes. Think about the effect of spending only a few minutes a day on a particular activity. For example, if you spend a few minutes a day reading ten pages of a book, you will read over a dozen books in a year. Similarly, dedicating as little as thirty minutes each day to exercise will produce an evident transformation in your physical health over a period of several months. Even writing just one page every day will tally up to a significant number of 365 pages in one year, which is ample content for a whole book. These are just some examples of how small, daily efforts can amount to a huge outcome.

The momentum factor comes into play in this process. As you settle into a routine and regularly partake in your preferred activities, you start developing a sense of momentum that keeps pushing you along. This building habit makes it more and more convenient to keep going, sometimes even resulting in progress that almost feels automatic. Soon enough, you will be realizing your aspirations and progressing in your pursuits without even needing to motivate yourself constantly, as the cadence of your routine takes you along.

The popular myth is that you need to wait for motivation to strike before you can set out on any endeavour. But motivation is usually a temporary thing, a spark which easily burns out. True strength of achievement, however, is discipline—the capability to act and get things done regardless of whether you are inspired or not. Motivation can give a short-term boost, but it is discipline that keeps you moving forward in the long term.

To help you understand the difference between these two principles, let me provide an example: motivation is similar to a flash of inspiration that makes you want to begin a project, telling yourself, "I'm feeling inspired, so I'll do it." Discipline, on the other hand, is the consistent determination to stick with it even after the initial enthusiasm wears off, causing you to tell yourself, "I'll do it, even though I don't feel like it." This difference alone shows how only using motivation can make you inconsistent and will end up stopping your progress in the long run. Looking back at my own experience, I started out full of enthusiasm as I embarked on fulfilling my objectives. But as the weeks went by, that initial enthusiasm gradually lost its grip, and I was confronted with the fact that motivation was not enough. It was then that I learned the strength of discipline. By creating structured routines, having reasonable daily goals, and being dedicated to appearing every day, I was able to sustain momentum. This single-minded commitment became the propellant for my success and revolutionized my methodology.

Creating consistency in your life is a process that takes deliberate effort with careful planning and dedication. It's important that you go into this endeavour with a strategic plan instead of waiting for things to happen on your own. A good step towards achieving this is working on small, manageable tasks. Rather than bogging yourself down with big dreams, divide your goals into small chunks of things that are actually possible for you to do on a daily basis. This incremental process not only builds a feeling of accomplishment but also sets the stage for greater change in the long run.

Developing a routine is another key factor in building consistency. As activities become routines in your daily routine, they automatically become habits that are less dependent on mental energy to sustain them. For example, allocating a specific time every morning to do a productive activity, such as reading, exercise, or learning, can go a long way towards increasing your consistency in doing it. By incorporating these habits into your everyday life, you develop a system that works in your Favor and helps you stay consistent.

Lastly, monitoring your progress is crucial to ensuring motivation and responsibility. Using methods like journals, apps, or calendars can help you see the path you've taken and enjoy your milestones, however small. It's also essential to detect and remove obstacles that can jeopardize your consistency. Whether too much time spent on social media or procrastination, being able to recognize them enables you to take action towards overcoming them. By establishing clear, defined objectives, you can guarantee that your actions are meaningful, and it becomes simpler to remain dedicated to your course of consistency.

The value of consistency goes far beyond personal growth; it is central to business, relationships, and nearly every part of our lives. In business, success is never an overnight experience. Business leaders who find great success do so due to a constant commitment, a desire to learn from setbacks, and an unwavering dedication to their vision. This constant chase not only brings development but also builds a profile of trustworthiness, a quality which plays a crucial role in building a strong market presence.

Trust is the foundation of customer loyalty, and consistency is the vehicle for establishing trust. When customers feel they can rely on a business for quality and service to be consistent, they will continue to come back time and again. This predictability instils a sense of security, allowing customers to develop long-term relationships with brands. In a competitive market, companies that focus on consistency in what they offer and how they engage are usually the ones that prosper, as they build a loyal customer base that appreciates their reliability.

In personal relationships, the basis of enduring relationships is not necessarily formed through lavish expressions of love but through the constant efforts made in the long term. Frequent talk, trust, and constant support are key factors that develop these relationships. Likewise, when seeking personal development, whether it is learning a new skill, getting healthier, or building new habits, it is the repetition and commitment that finally result in mastery and change. Committing to consistency in every aspect of life can result in deep and long-term alterations, enhancing both personal and professional lives.

One of the greatest examples of consistency resulting in astounding success is that of Stephen King, the highly productive writer who is famous for his thrilling books. King is a stickler for his writing schedule, generating a whopping 2,000 words daily without fail. This steadfast dedication to his work has seen him publish more than 60 novels and hundreds of short stories, demonstrating what can be achieved through a rigorous approach to writing. His dedication is a testament to the strength of habit and the value of turning up every day to work on one's craft.

Dwayne "The Rock" Johnson is the perfect example of how a good work ethic can take a person to the top. Sure, his natural ability and charm play a part in his popularity, but it is his unwavering dedication to regular training and hard work that has made him one of the highest-paid stars in Hollywood. Johnson's daily routine consists of intense exercises and a strict lifestyle, proving that success is usually the result of unceasing effort and determination rather than talent alone. His transition from a professional wrestler to an international superstar in itself highlights the importance of consistency in realizing one's dreams.

Serena Williams is the best example of how hard work and regular practice can take a person to heights of greatness in sports. From her glorious tennis career, Williams has not just depended on her natural ability but has also been committed to a tough training routine that focuses on hard work and determination. Her diligence in constant improvement and her tenacious search for excellence have endeared her as one of the greatest sports figures in history. Williams' tale shows that success is not just a result of a person's abilities; it is the outcome of unshakeable commitment and the desire to work hard day after day.

Inconsistency can sneakily destroy your dreams and derailed your path to success. When you do not stick to your objectives, the implications can be drastic. One of the most tangible impacts is lost momentum; every time you stall or deviate from your course, you not only lose the ground you have gained but also make it harder to get back to your old rhythm. This cycle of starting and stopping can create a frustrating barrier that hinders your ability to move forward.

Additionally, the emotional cost of inconsistency can result in frustration and self-doubt. When your actions fail to produce the desired outcome, it's easy to get discouraged. This discouragement can snowball into a loss of confidence in your capabilities, making it even harder to commit again to your objectives. The psychological battle of doubting your value and potential can be a major obstacle on your path, further hindering your way to success.

Also, inconsistency can lead to lost opportunities that come about with consistent effort and commitment. If you are consistently working towards your goals, you might miss opportunities for development, cooperation, or progress that could have been yours if you had remained committed. The take home is crystal clear: actual success does not come about through spotty effort but through constant repetition of the right actions over a period of time. Adopting this attitude can change your strategy and take you to the success you want.

Creating consistency in your habits can be a life-changing process, and there are a number of useful exercises that can assist you in the process. One good approach is to undertake a 30-day challenge in which you choose a particular habit to develop, for example, exercising, reading, or spending time on a personal project. The trick is to stick with this habit on a daily basis for a period of one month, leaving zero space for excuses. This narrow focus not only aids in making the habit a part of yourself but also fortifies your commitment and willpower as you can see your achievements over time.

Another helpful tactic is the 2-Minute Rule, which challenges you to approach overwhelming tasks by committing to only two minutes of work. This small investment of time tends to create a momentum that makes it more comfortable to continue beyond the initial two minutes. Furthermore, involving an accountability partner can make a huge difference in your level of dedication; by getting someone on board who can encourage and periodically check in on you, you establish a system of two-way motivation. Finally, monitoring your streak—whether by paper calendar or computer app—can be a potent motivator. Every time you're able to maintain your habit during the day, crossing it off gives a mental image of how committed you are, helping to keep you engaged and motivated.

There are no shortcuts or magic spells in the path to success. It is beyond luck or natural ability; it is more a matter of your daily devotion to your dreams. Every day offers a chance to invest in your future, and it is by this constant drive that you are able to really make headway. The essence of success lies in the ability to show up, put in the necessary effort, and remain steadfast in your pursuit of goals, regardless of the challenges that may arise.

Consistency is the key bridge that ties your present to your future. It is a potent tool that can turn dreams into reality. Rather than waiting for perfect conditions or depending on momentary motivation, take charge and start today. Accept the journey, stay on course through the highs and lows, and see the incredible transformations that take place in your life as you take one conscious step after another.

Reflection Questions for the Reader:

1. What is one area of my life where I need to be more consistent?
2. What small, daily action can I start today that will bring me closer to my goals?
3. How can I stay disciplined even when motivation runs out?

Chapter 6

Smart work in the right direction matters more than just hard work

The ubiquitous phrase "put in the work and success will be yours" is something we've all heard, but it's also important to remember that plain old hard work isn't always the only answer to success. You could work around the clock for months on end on your assignments, but if you lack direction or strategy, you're more likely to be seeing very little return. This is where working smart comes in, as it focuses on the need to make your efforts align with your goals.

Working smart entails an emphasis on efficiency, strategy, and purpose. It's about maximizing your time, energy, and resources to drive you toward your vision in a smarter way. What we're going to cover in this chapter is how to integrate hard work with smart planning to help you boost your productivity and realize your aspirations faster and better.

Comprehending the Idea of Smart Work Smart work goes beyond the idea of working long hours; it is about working more smartly. It means focusing on high-impact activities and using creative and effective techniques to achieve your goals. In contrast to productivity measurement in terms of hours worked, intelligent work targets the quality and efficiency of work being performed to ensure that all efforts count positively towards the desired results.

Differentiating Hard Work from Smart Work Differentiating between hard work and smart work is quite pertinent. Hard work generally involves putting in long hours and putting a lot of effort, but it might not always result in the best outcomes. On the other hand, smart work involves planning and prioritization, relying on different tools and techniques in order to improve productivity. This is what sets apart the fact that working harder is not always equivalent to working smarter, but instead, it's about maximizing resources and efforts in order to deliver the optimal outcomes.

A Practical Example To understand the distinction, imagine two people who have been asked to dig a hole. One individual uses a conventional shovel and toils away all day (embodying hard work), while the other person decides to hire an excavator and finishes the job within one hour (standing for smart work). While both are doing the same thing, the second one illustrates how using the correct tools and methods can result in much more productive outcomes, highlighting the very spirit of smart work at work.

The Need for Smart Work It is imperative that you do smart work to achieve maximum productivity and efficiency. When you follow a strategic method in doing your task, you are able to complete more work within a minimal time frame, freeing you to focus on other important endeavours. Not only does this technique increase your productivity, but it also leaves room for personal development and recreation, which are important for living life to the fullest.

Relieving Stress and Improving Results A disorganized work approach tends to result in burnout and crippling stress. Intelligent work avoids these dangers by promoting a concentration on high-priority activities that really count. By focusing your energy on what matters most, you can produce better results with less effort, ultimately leading to a healthier work-life balance and a more rewarding career experience.

Smart Working Strategies in Order to Work Smartly To work smartly, it is important to have well-defined and achievable goals that direct your endeavours. Prioritizing your work according to the importance of each task can determine which tasks will bring you the most returns so that you can use your time effectively. Further, the application of technology and dividing big objectives into small steps that you can take can simplify your workflow, making complex projects less overwhelming. Learning from other people's successes can also give you useful information, allowing you to implement tested methods that are consistent with your goals.

The power to focus in the distraction-filled world of today is like having a superpower. Instead of trying to do more, the key to productive work is to focus on what is important and reduce involvement in less important tasks. By focusing on key tasks, people can get more done with less effort, elevating their productivity levels.

In order to improve concentration, it is important to remove distractions that have the potential to derail your attention. This can be done by disabling notifications on gadgets, setting clear boundaries about your availability, and creating a workspace that promotes an environment that is conducive to concentration. A clean and organized space can go a long way in improving your capacity to focus on the task at hand, enabling deeper involvement and more substantial work.

Another fundamental element of productive focus is the discipline of single-tasking rather than multitasking. Although it might appear efficient to do many things at once, it actually results in less productivity and more mistakes. By focusing your mind on one thing at a time, you are able to get better results. Also, using time blocking—dividing certain blocks of time to specific tasks—can further optimize your workflow to ensure that you are always investing time in your most important responsibilities. This planned method not only maximizes organization but also makes you more likely to stick with what really succeeds.

Within business, adopting smart work can substantially boost productivity and fuel growth. One of the best ways to do this is by automating routine tasks using technology and computer software. Through this method, you save precious time, and you can focus on creating groundbreaking strategies that steer your business into growth. With less time being used for boring tasks, you can channel your energy into more meaningful projects that promote growth and success.

The second important skill of smart work in a business setting is the art of delegating. It's important to know that trying to do all the work by yourself can result in burnout and inefficiency. By delegating tasks to the team members who have the required skills and experience, you not only give them empowerment but also make your work environment more dynamic and efficient. This strategic delegation guarantees that activities are done better, enabling you to concentrate on more strategic decision-making and planning.

Outside of the workplace, smart work is also crucial in personal life. Maintaining a healthy work-life balance is of utmost importance, and embracing smart work values can enable you to attain your personal objectives without sacrificing your well-being. Moreover, pledging to ongoing learning is crucial; by setting aside time to learn new skills and knowledge, you become more efficient and responsive. This constant quest for development not only enhances your individual life but also prepares you with the skills required to deal with the intricacies of work and life more easily.

Bill Gates is the model of smart work as he set the tone for smart work by having a vision-driven problem-solving mindset. Instead of just working long hours, Gates focused on strategic innovation and utilizing technology efficiently, which was instrumental in propelling Microsoft to great heights. His vision to read the market trend and respond to it enabled him to design solutions that not only met current problems but also projected into the future, demonstrating the potential of astute work leading to gigantic achievements.

Elon Musk is yet another best example of an individual who personifies the concept of smart work. He uses a technique called First Principles Thinking, where he breaks down intricate issues into their basic elements. In this way, Musk can spot the most effective and creative solutions, which frequently result in revolutionary breakthroughs in technology and business. His method focuses on comprehending the essence of a problem instead of following established beliefs, enabling him to break new ground and achieve astounding outcomes.

Tim Ferriss has made a serious mark on working smarter with his number one bestseller, The 4-Hour Workweek. He pushes the idea of mindset change by prompting people to prioritize automation, delegating work, and selecting high-impact tasks. Focusing on the truly important stuff and cutting the crap, Ferriss has opened people's minds and encouraged people around the globe to change the way they view productivity, that being smarter working leads to improved efficiency and happiness.

Working tirelessly without a solid plan can have severe consequences. The biggest danger is burnout, a condition of physical and emotional exhaustion that leaves you drained and uninspired. When you invest your energy in activities without a plan, the constant grind can wear down your mental well-being, and it becomes hard to stay motivated and enthusiastic about your work.

Moreover, investing effort in your work without a strategic direction can result in wasted energy and resources. You might end up spending hours on end on activities that do not produce significant outcomes, just because you are not setting the right goals. This lack of alignment can form a frustrating loop where you are busy but not productive, eventually slowing down your progress and achievement.

In addition, an absence of strategic analysis can lead to stagnation, whereby you are still in the same place even with your efforts. Without periodically checking your approach and results, you may end up stuck in a pattern that yields little development or progress. This can be especially demotivating, as the long hours you put in might not be equated with the advancement you hope for, making you feel stagnant and unaccomplished in your pursuits.

Hard work without a specific purpose is like the pointless act of running on a treadmill; you might be losing energy and logging the time, but you're back where you started, making no actual progress. This simile points out the need to have a specific goal or direction for your efforts. Without a guide to direct your efforts, all the hard work and effort can create a feeling of frustration, realizing that no matter how hard you work, you are not moving closer to your desired goals. It's necessary to direct your hard work towards worthwhile activities that are aligned with your dreams, so each step you make moves you closer to your final destination.

In order to start on a path of working smarter, start with an exhaustive task audit. Take the time to record all the activities you perform throughout your day. This activity will assist you in distinguishing which things are absolutely necessary to your goals and which activities can be assigned to others, automated by technology, or eliminated altogether. With this clarity on your daily tasks, you can organize your efforts and concentrate on what really matters.

Second, adopt the 80/20 principle, a very potent rule that encourages you to think that the majority of your results stem from a minority of your actions. Review your objectives and identify the 20% of activities that will produce 80% of the outcomes you seek. By focusing your energy on these high-impact tasks, you can drive maximum productivity and see to it that your time is dedicated to actions that make important contributions toward your goals.

Lastly, it should be a regular practice to reflect weekly. After every week, spend some time reviewing your success and questioning yourself: "Did I work smart this week? What are some strategies that I can implement in order to maximize my efficiency from now on?" This reflective process not only supports ongoing improvement but also keeps you on track with your goals so that you are focused and effective in your pursuits.

On the path to success, hard work alone should not be the focus; instead, one must focus on working wisely and intentionally. With the union of constant effort and careful planning, you will be able to achieve your goals more quickly and efficiently. This way, you are better equipped to deal with obstacles, making your efforts bring the highest returns.

It's important to note that the amount of time spent on activities is not as important as the quality of the time. Focus on high-impact tasks, prioritize your time wisely, and always look for chances to improve how you do things. Adopting this frame of mind is essential to unleashing your true potential and accomplishing the success you desire.

Reflection Questions for the Reader:

1. Am I working hard but not seeing the results I want? Where can I apply smarter strategies?
2. What tools or techniques can I use to be more efficient in my work?
3. How can I better prioritize my tasks to focus on what really matters?

Chapter 7

Books are your best friends—they hold the knowledge of the world

Imagine yourself in a conversation with some of the greatest minds ever—visionaries, scholars, innovators, and leaders. What if you were able to tap into their wisdom, learn from their setbacks, and draw on their experience to enrich your own path? That is what books do for us.

Well beyond simple gatherings of printed pages, books are transformative tools that have the power to change your thinking, promote self-improvement, and guide you toward success. In this chapter, we will explore the deep meaning of books, how they work as precious friends throughout your life journey, offering not only knowledge but also inspiration and guidance.

The Worth of Books Over and Above Information Books are portals to a whole range of ideas and concepts, which enable you to visit areas that you might not have the opportunity to do so in everyday life. Reading opens your mind, challenging your assumptions and making you think about things from different perspectives. This mental broadening not only enriches your perspective on the world but also teaches you to empathize because you begin to see and value the variety of experiences and cultures that colour human life.

Books as Always-Available Counsellors Picture having a personal guru at your fingertips, willing and able to impart knowledge whenever the need arises. Books do that perfectly well, providing insights by great minds across all walks of life. Whether you are gaining insight into the strategic brain of a business innovator or being taught profound principles of life from a legendary author, every page becomes a meeting with a coach who can see you through rough times and spur you on towards your highest capability, without ever being held down by the bonds of time and space.

The Inspiration of the Page A thoughtfully written sentence or an intriguing story can become deeply resonating, inspiring action and fuelling passion in you. The examples of people overcoming difficulties or succeeding against all odds remind us dramatically of what it is possible to do. These stories not only inspire persistence but also infuse a sense of hope, challenging you to pursue your aspirations and overcome challenges with new Vigor. Thus, books become not only means of education, but motivators for personal transformation, advancement, and becoming an instrument of positive change in society.

The benefits of reading are vast, and they can actually be described as a tremendous resource in our lives. Among the greatest is the knowledge you gain. The more information you accumulate from reading, the better equipped you become to make good decisions. Books are portals to knowing about the different facets of life and enterprise, preparing you with the insight needed to drive through challenging issues and dilemmas.

In a time filled with distractions, reading is one of the great aids to increase concentration and concentration. Reading calls for focused attention, which condition your mind for staying focused over a long stretch of time. The capacity for concentration is not only helpful for individual pursuits but also in working life, where the ability to remain focused may make all the difference in an active setting.

In addition, reading greatly improves your communication skills. It makes you more articulate and better able to understand, enabling you to convey your ideas and thoughts with clarity and confidence. Whether you are presenting or conversing on a daily basis, being able to communicate is a huge plus. Moreover, reading makes you more imaginative and creative problem-solver since it exposes you to different thinking and creative possibilities, as well as offering the much-needed relaxation that can cure stress and soothe your soul.

Books exist in a multitude of genres, each with their own special insights and advantages that can make our lives better in one way or another. Self-help and personal development books are especially effective, as they give readers the tools and techniques they need to improve their lives. These books tend to concentrate on developing good habits, improving self-esteem, and personal development. A good example is Stephen Covey's "The 7 Habits of Highly Effective People," which presents vital principles for attaining personal and professional effectiveness, leading readers towards a more rewarding life.

In business and entrepreneurship, literature is an important tool for prospective leaders and entrepreneurs. The books explore the ins and outs of beginning and running a business, providing useful insights on financial planning and leadership strategies. "Rich Dad Poor Dad" by Robert Kiyosaki is the exception here, as it compares various money philosophies and inspires readers to adopt a mindset focused on building wealth and achieving financial freedom. Such information can prove priceless to anyone who wants to understand the intricacies of the business world.

Literature and fiction, although viewed by some as purely entertainment, are significant in the cultivation of creativity and empathy. Through reading and narratives, people are immersed in different worlds and outlooks, enabling them to live vicariously through others. One good example is the literature work of Harper Lee, "To Kill a Mockingbird," which tackles deeper social issues and human ethics, making readers question their own values and beliefs. Moreover, science and philosophy books question our perception of the universe and stimulate critical thinking. "Sapiens: A Brief History of Humankind" by Yuval Noah Harari asks readers to discover the history of humanity, challenging conventional norms and stimulating further reflection on our position in the world.

My reading life started later in life, and it was a life-changing experience that rewrote my worldview. At first, I used to see books as just information packs, but when I started reading titles about life, business, and self-help, I realized their full potential. These stories and lessons made me see the deep influence literature can have on personal growth and development.

Among the numerous books I read, there was one that proved to be a turning point: Napoleon Hill's "Think and Grow Rich." This book taught me the fundamental principles of how to develop a positive attitude, define detailed objectives, and exhibit relentless perseverance. The lessons I learned from Hill's teachings became crucial in overcoming the obstacles I encountered, enabling me to overcome obstacles and chase my dreams with renewed Vigor.

Ever since that transformative experience, I have ensured reading becomes part of my regular schedule. Every book I read brings new ideas and lessons, sparking my urge for ongoing learning. The information that I get not only widens my world understanding but also stimulates me to take action, validating the concept that literature can be a powerful catalyst for change in our existence.

Building a reading habit can be a fulfilling experience, and it's crucial to start with small steps. Rather than bogging yourself down with the prospect of reading an entire book at one sitting, try committing 10 pages or 15 minutes a day to reading. This incremental method not only makes the task less intimidating but also enables you to create a sustainable habit that can yield tremendous progress in the long run.

The secret to finding reading enjoyable is to choose books that really interest you. Whether you find yourself attracted to exciting adventures, astute business plans, or inspiring personal growth tales, picking subjects that appeal to you will make the activity much more pleasant. When reading is a delight and not an obligation, you will be more inclined to continue with it and venture into new concepts and opinions.

Having specific goals for your reading can be a great motivator in your literary life. By holding yourself to the goal of reading a certain number of books per month or per year, you give yourself a sense of direction and accomplishment. Also, having a set reading routine—a daily one in the early morning, an hour or so during breaks at work, or a soothing one before bed—can make you even more committed. To reinforce your learning, try taking notes and reflecting on what you have read, as this activity not only supports your learning but also assists you in implementing new knowledge into your life.

The power of reading is enormous, but it is through action that that power is converted into real achievements. Reading should not be a passive activity; it should be a force that brings change into your life, both personal and professional. The secret to getting the most out of reading is to take the learning that you do and actually apply it to your day-to-day life and decision-making.

In order to properly apply the lessons learned through your reading, try applying a single concept at a time. Once you finish a book, find one thing that stands out to you the most and set about implementing it in your life. By keeping it to a single concept at a time, you can explore the ramifications of that idea to its fullest potential, which helps you notice the effect and refine your strategies from there.

Also, passing on your acquired knowledge to others can greatly help improve your understanding. Through teaching or explaining what you have learned, you reinforce your understanding of the subject matter and cement the lessons in your mind. Moreover, some books are worth reading again; re-reading them can reveal underlying meanings and new insights, enhancing your understanding and widening your intellectual perspectives.

The redemptive power of literature is dramatically depicted in the life of Oprah Winfrey, who credits her ascension from poverty to the transformative influence of books in her life. Her love for reading not only expanded her horizons but also drove her ambition, culminating in the creation of Oprah's Book Club. This program has encouraged millions of people to adopt reading, creating a culture of readers who share the experience of discovery and self-improvement.

Elon Musk is an excellent example of how reading and self-study can lead to amazing accomplishments. When asked how he was an expert in rocket science, Musk simply replied, "I read books." This answer reinforces the point that what is learned through reading can inspire people to create and break the Mold of what can be achieved, as Musk has done with space travel and technology.

Microsoft co-founder Bill Gates is a prime example of the power of lifelong learning through books, reading around 50 books per year and being committed to such an endeavour. Gates feels that the knowledge and ideas he gained from reading these books have played a crucial role in his success. Gates' dedication to lifelong learning through books not only signifies his own personal development but also the wider implication of reading as a means for intellectual growth and success in multiple areas.

One of the most common excuses for not reading is that there just isn't enough time in the day. But the reality is that you don't have to spend long periods of time reading; even five to ten minutes can add up to a lot of reading over the course of time. Try replacing some of your social media browsing with a few pages of a book. This minor adjustment can easily incorporate reading into your daily life, making it a more convenient and enjoyable habit.

Another typical excuse is the feeling that reading is not attractive. This usually comes from not having found the right material that speaks to you. The world of literature is enormous, with an infinite number of genres and styles, so it's a good idea to take the time to try out various kinds of books. Whether fiction, non-fiction, fantasy, or mystery, discovering a book that engages your interest can change your attitude towards reading from a burden to a pleasant getaway.

Other readers complain of their inability to retain what they have read, discouraging them from ever again reaching for a book. In counteracting this, use measures such as taking notes, marking essential parts of the book, or discussing the contents with others, either book clubs or friends. Not only does this increase one's chances of retaining, but it also allows one to learn more in-depth and appreciate the work further, hence a better experience from the reading process.

Reading can be a life-changing activity, and there are a few useful exercises to assist you in making the most of this enriching practice. One helpful method is to prepare your own reading list. Spend a bit of time writing down 5 to 10 books that have interested you throughout your lifespan. By establishing a specific target to finish these books within a specified timeframe, you give yourself a purpose and motivation that can drive you towards achieving your reading goals.

Another great means of maximizing your reading experience is through joining a book club or reading group. This collective atmosphere not only breeds responsibility but allows for the access to lively debates that can serve to heighten your appreciation and comprehension of the material. Engaging with fellow readers can reveal aspects of the books that would otherwise not be considered, thus enriching the overall experience and appreciation of the literature.

Finally, think about tracking your reading experience through journaling. Once you have completed each book, sit down and think about the main points and how they apply to your life. This not only reinforces your learning but also makes you think critically about the themes and lessons of the book. And if your time is limited, incorporating audiobooks into your schedule can be a lifesaver. Whether you are traveling to work or exercising, listening to books enables you to maximize your time while still enjoying the world of books.

In short, books are precious tools for self-improvement and self-awareness. They are not just hobbies; they are constant companions that walk with you through life, providing insights, generating curiosity, and challenging you to broaden your perspectives. If you are looking for motivation, wisdom, or a new perspective, the written word has an incredible power to redefine your knowledge of the world and yourself.

So, don't wait to get immersed in that book you've been eager to investigate. Welcome the friendship of literature, and you will discover it can open doors to experiences and possibilities you never thought possible. By making books a part of your life, you lay the groundwork for rich personal development and change.

Reflection Questions for the Reader:

1. What book has had the biggest impact on my life so far?
2. How can I make reading a regular part of my daily routine?
3. What's one lesson from a book that I can apply to my life or business today?

Chapter 8

Be your best every day to become the best version of yourself

The journey to achieving your best life is one on which many desire to walk, as everyone is drawn to the goal of succeeding, being happy, and being fulfilled. The critical question, though, is: What are you doing every day to make those dreams a reality? Success is not just one event; instead, it is a daily commitment to personal betterment. Every day offers a new opportunity to improve your skills, add to your knowledge, and take another step in the direction of the person you see yourself being. In this chapter, we will explore how small, consistent steps can dramatically affect your own personal change in the long term.

Here, it is not about reaching perfection but more about the process of progression. With every daily endeavour, no matter how insignificant, you are able to instil notable change within yourself. In this exploration, persistence will be shown as essential, along with the cumulative value of your day-to-day choices, eventually leading you toward a happier and more prosperous life.

Being your best is more than being perfect or better than someone else. It's about individual improvement and self-betterment. It's about deliberately trying to be a better person than you were yesterday. This process is about taking an active role in your own growth, committing yourself to your objectives, and accepting the challenges that arise.

Central to this pursuit is the value of effort. It's necessary to put all that you have and focus all your energy and attention into your endeavours, whether professional or personal. Growth is also a fundamental aspect; it means introspection about your experiences, learning from failures, and constantly looking for means to increase your skills and knowledge. The dedication to become a better version of yourself is what keeps moving you forward in your journey.

Consistency is key in becoming your best self. It means being present every day despite challenges or exhaustion. Authenticity is also important; it entails staying true to yourself and your values while loving your own self for who you are. By combining these values into your life, you are building a strong foundation for growth and satisfaction that ultimately guides you toward the best version of yourself.

The importance of aiming for excellence every day cannot be overemphasized. Each minor success you gain forms part of a greater fabric of success. These little achievements, taken for granted, build up over time and lay the foundation for great success. By paying attention to these small achievements, you prime yourself for greater ones, affirming the fact that every attempt matters and can culminate in phenomenal results.

Continuously doing your best creates a feeling of improvement that is necessary for self-development. With each success you see the results of, your confidence starts to grow, and this creates a positive feedback loop that increases your drive to do more. This energy is what you need; it pushes you to keep going, motivating you to challenge yourself further with determination. The more you put into your daily work, the more you develop a growth-oriented and resilient mindset that welcomes change.

In an uncertain world, what you can control is all that matters. Although what happens around you is not in your control, your attitude each day and how hard you work are all yours to command. By exercising commitment to excellence, you are not just making your life better but also giving it meaning and purpose. This purposeful strategy turns your day-to-day activities from existence to a fulfilling experience, enabling you to build a life consistent with your values and desires.

To maximize your potential each day, it's essential to begin with a structured approach. Establishing daily objectives can provide clarity and direction. Aim for small, manageable targets that contribute to your larger aspirations. For instance, if your goal is to launch a business, dedicate time to analyse your competitors or draft a section of your business plan. This concentrated effort not only keeps you inspired but also guarantees that you are continually moving towards your final vision.

How you start your morning can greatly determine the rest of your day. Developing a morning routine that energizes you is key to having a good beginning. Wake up slightly early to add activities that get your mind and body moving, such as doing some physical exercise, reading for a short while, or writing down your goals for the day ahead. This deliberate beginning can boost your productivity and create a sense of achievement from the very start.

Prioritization is the most important thing when it comes to efficiently managing your daily activities. Focus on the tasks that bring the most output by using the 80/20 rule, which states that 80% of your results are generated by only 20% of your efforts. Moreover, developing a habit of gratitude can also add more depth to your daily life. By spending a moment writing down three things you're thankful for, either at the beginning or end of your day, you're able to keep a positive outlook. Lastly, looking back over your day's successes and what you can do better enables you to evolve and improve, ensuring that you continue to stay focused on your goals.

Embracing the path of self-improvement is not an easy task, particularly when life presents unexpected obstacles your way. It's crucial to remember that not every day will be a brilliant one; some days will be weighed down with tiredness, lack of motivation, or even disappointment. The secret to getting through these difficult periods is realizing that seeking perfection is not the goal. Rather, seek consistency in your efforts. On those tough days, resolve to get at least one small thing done that moves you ahead, however insignificant it might be.

When confronted with huge responsibilities, breaking down the bigger tasks into smaller, easy-to-handle segments can be of help. Apart from making a frightening project look less daunting, this also makes it possible to enjoy incremental accomplishments. Every single step you achieve is a victory on its own, adding up to your big journey. By concentrating on these bite-sized accomplishments, you can sustain a sense of momentum and motivation even when the larger picture seems distant.

The people that you surround yourself with have a great impact on your capacity to endure difficulties. Being among supportive and positive people can develop a good environment that helps you grow and be more resilient. These are the kind of relationships that can be a source of inspiration, reminding you of your potential and encouraging you to do your best. Also, when motivation is lagging behind, it's important to reconnect with your underlying purpose. Looking back at the reasons that first drove you will remind you of your enthusiasm and motivation, so you can move through the challenges with new Vigor.

Michael Jordan was a giant figure in the realm of basketball and is frequently ranked as one of the greatest ever to play the game. Though his path to greatness was never just about being naturally gifted, it was that he never wavered from continuing to improve as an individual athlete that made the difference. Jordan was famous for his rigorous practice regimen, many times out-doing his training partners. He accepted challenges and tried to challenge his limits, proving that success is the result of hard work and a constant pursuit of excellence.

J.K. Rowling's journey to literary fame is an inspiring one of perseverance and determination. Prior to becoming a household name with the Harry Potter books, Rowling encountered several setbacks, such as having her work rejected by publishers several times who could not envision the future success of her books. Instead of being discouraged, she never gave up on refining her skill, investing her heart in her craft and believing in the magic of her tale. Her unrelenting dedication to her vision eventually made her one of the most popular writers in contemporary literature.

Dwayne "The Rock" Johnson's transformation from a college football player to an international entertainment superstar is the epitome of the strength of hard work and perseverance. His path is characterized by an unwavering dedication to self-improvement, both physically and mentally. Johnson often stresses the value of consistency in his work, whether at the gym or in his career. His life is a poignant reminder that determination and a commitment to ongoing improvement will lead one to achieve great success in many aspects.

Daily habits cannot be overemphasized; they form the foundation of a successful life. The apparently insignificant actions that you engage in daily set the platform for your future success. By developing a routine, you provide a platform on which success can grow, given that these habits tend to accumulate over time and result in serious outcomes.

One of the effective ways to create new habits is habit stacking, where a new behaviour is coupled with an existing one. For example, you can choose to spend five minutes planning your daily goals as soon as you brush your teeth in the morning. This strategy does not just make it easy to adopt new habits but also helps them become part of your normal routine.

Tracking your progress is also an important part of habit creation. Keeping a journal or using a specific app to monitor your habits can give you a visual image of your progress, helping you stay motivated as you see yourself improve. Don't also forget to reward yourself for reaching small milestones throughout the process. Rewarding yourself for these wins reinforces good behaviour and motivates you to keep going on the road to success.

Aiming for excellence every day does not mean pushing yourself to the point of burnout. It is important to discover a balanced coexistence between your goals and the necessary practice of self-care. Understanding that your physical and mental health are more important can help you adopt a more sustainable model for reaching your goals. Prioritizing rest and recovery gives you the chance to recharge, which in turn makes you more productive and creative.

Practicing mindfulness can largely enhance your concentration and lower the stress levels. By focusing on the moment at hand and completely engaging in your present tasks, you can develop a clearer mind that enables better performance. Mindfulness not only assists in the control of anxiety but also promotes better engagement with your work, which becomes more enjoyable and rewarding. This clarity of mind can be a great ally in dealing with the pitfalls of ambition.

Having a successful career is but one aspect of a happy life. It is crucial to make time for personal relationships, interests, and downtime. A balanced life, in which work and personal interests are both present, not only makes your experiences richer but also leads to long-term success. By developing different areas of your life, you build a foundation that sustains your goals while keeping you grounded and satisfied.

Taking the self-improvement journey can result in deep changes that go beyond your work life and find their way into all areas of your life. By becoming the best version of yourself every day, you start to observe huge changes in your thinking and behaviour. This dedication creates a growth mindset, where you see challenges as a means of learning instead of obstacles. Through life's challenges and triumphs, you develop resilience and flexibility, which are critical qualities for success in both personal and career life.

Aside from individual development, the pursuit of excellence also improves your relationships with other people. Through the practice of values like empathy, honesty, and integrity, you establish a positive atmosphere where there is free communication and mutual trust. Not only does this improve your relationship with friends, family, and co-workers but also motivates others to aim higher. When you show up as the real you with others, you create a connection of community and belonging that will enrich your existence and the lives of the people you encounter.

Ultimately, striving to be your best self creates a deep feeling of fulfilment and purpose. By aligning your actions with your values and desires, you feel a stronger sense of purpose and connection to your life's calling. Alignment creates a deeper feeling of satisfaction, as you feel that you are living truthfully and making a positive difference in the world around you. The path of self-betterment is not merely about personal accomplishment; it is about living a life full of purpose, happiness, and dedication to ongoing development.

Engaging in practical exercises can significantly enhance your journey toward becoming the best version of yourself. One effective method is to maintain a daily reflection journal. This involves taking a few moments each day to jot down your accomplishments, identify areas for improvement, and express gratitude for something positive in your life. This exercise not only helps in building self-awareness but also brings with it a mindset of appreciation and growth, so you are able to acknowledge your progress and plan for the future.

Another effective tool is the development of a vision board. This visual summary of your dreams can be used as inspiration and encouragement. By collecting images, quotes, and symbols that are meaningful to what you want and dream of, you have something tangible to remind you of what you are working towards. Positioning this board in an accessible place functions as a constant reminder to stay mindful of your goals every day, reminding you to remain cantered and motivated along your journey to self-enhancement.

Also, try taking on the "Best Self" challenge, where you pledge to create a new habit for a month. This can be anything from adding exercise into your daily routine to setting aside time every day for reading or practicing gratitude. To go along with this challenge, have a weekly check-in where you review your progress, acknowledge your successes, and create new goals for the upcoming week. This disciplined way of being not only makes you accountable, but it enables you to evolve and improve on your personal growth consistently.

The key to personal growth is not about being perfect, but about being dedicated to improvement. To be the best version of yourself is to be on the journey of improvement, where every day is an opportunity to show up and put your energy into becoming better. It's about being committed to the process, even when things get tough, and knowing that every little step in the right direction counts towards your overall growth.

Remember that achievement is not a destination, but a continuous journey with room for learning and growth. Every day presents a new opportunity to line up your behaviour with your goals, to do your best, and to move a little bit closer to the life you desire. Meet each day with purpose, fully immerse yourself in your endeavours, and observe the extraordinary miracle that happens as you become the best version of yourself.

Reflection Questions for the Reader:

1. What does being my best self-look like to me?
2. What small habits can I start today to improve myself?
3. How can I stay motivated and consistent, even when life gets tough?

Chapter 9

Problems are not obstacles; they are steps toward success

Introduction: Shifting Your Attitude toward Challenges How do you handle life's challenges? Do you view them as insurmountable obstacles that are stopping you in your tracks, or do you see them as opportunities for personal and professional growth? Most people have a tendency to view challenges as negative occurrences to be avoided. But what if I told you that these challenges are actually concealed opportunities? They are not intended to be obstacles on your path; instead, they are there to teach you, Shape your character, and prepare you for the next step of your life and career.

In this chapter, we'll delve into the deep influence of changing your attitude towards challenges, showing how a change in mindset can turn stumbling blocks into important stepping stones to success. Through adopting a mentality that sees challenges as necessary learning experiences, you can tap into new levels of resilience and resourcefulness. This method not only improves your capacity to handle challenges but also promotes a better appreciation of your potential, ultimately resulting in higher accomplishments in your personal and professional life.

The Role of Obstacles in Finding Success Challenges act as drivers for personal and professional growth. With every challenge they face, individuals are forced out of their comfort zones, promoted to think out of the box and learn new skills.

Without these obstacles, the potential for real growth lessens considerably because it is only through overcoming them that we become better.

Challenges Build Resilience Fighting and surmounting challenges builds a strong mental strength. Every challenge that you overcome not only improves your capacity to deal with adversity but also gives you the strength that you need to face upcoming challenges. This process of problem-solving builds up your resilience, making you even more capable of dealing with whatever comes your way, ultimately readying you for even bigger challenges later on.

Challenges Bring Out Creativity Several revolutionary innovations and business startups have been the result of the need to overcome critical issues. With a challenge before them, people are compelled to go out of the box and develop creative solutions. What is more, how one responds to such challenges may also expose their true nature as they demonstrate traits like patience, perseverance, and determination, which are crucial for long-term success.

Shifting Your Mindset: Seeing Challenges as Opportunities Each challenge offers a one-of-a-kind chance for learning and development. Rather than getting bogged down in the question, "Why is this happening to me?" try reframing your mindset to ask, "What is the valuable lesson I can learn from this experience?" This change in mindset enables you to meet challenges with curiosity and resilience, allowing you to discover insights that can drive you forward.

Prioritize Solutions Over Problems It's far too easy to get bogged down in the problem itself, but this is what can hold you back.

Switch your attention away from the issue at hand to the solutions on the horizon. By seeking solutions proactively to problems instead of bemoaning them, not only do you cultivate a healthier attitude, but you also propel yourself forward that much faster to success. The sooner you move from a complaining state to an action state, the more empowered you will be to overcome challenges.

Embracing Failure as a Stepping Stone Instead of seeing failure as a step back, accept it as part of your path towards success. Every mistake provides a valuable lesson that can lead you further towards your dreams. With the understanding that failure is not the opposite of success but part of the process, you foster resilience and further insight into your journey. With a growth mindset, you are able to view your potential as an area that can be developed and increased with hard work and experience, turning obstacles into thrilling opportunities for growth.

The life of Thomas Edison is an inspiring example of the strength of persistence in the face of failure. Prior to successfully inventing the lightbulb, Edison had experienced more than a thousand failures. When contemplating these failures, he is famously quoted as saying that he hadn't failed but instead found a thousand ways that didn't work. This unflinching resolve turned what would have otherwise been perceived as insurmountable hurdles into one of the greatest inventions the world has ever known, demonstrating how resilience can culminate in revolutionary success.

Oprah Winfrey's life is an inspiring tale of adversity conquered and challenges as stepping stones to victory. Born poor and having had many challenges along the way, such as being let go from her initial television job, Oprah would not allow these to define her. Rather, she took the experiences gained through adversity and used them to move forward, eventually creating a media empire and inspiring millions. Her path depicts how accepting adversity can bring extraordinary achievements and impact.

The original founders of Airbnb best illustrate the innovation and perseverance in the face of failure. First, they faced a series of blunt rejection comments from would-be investors, which could have simply derailed them. Instead, however, instead of letting these setbacks get the best of them, they changed their approach, learned from their failures, and continued going. This determination proved to be worthwhile, as they made Airbnb a multi-billion-dollar company, proving that the road to success is most likely lined with challenges that may be conquered with ingenuity and willpower.

In order to convert problems into possibilities for success, the initial step is to identify the root problem instead of solving the symptoms at the surface. By exploring the problem at its core, you are able to discover the actual factors involved, which will help you come up with better solutions. For example, if your company is not growing, it's necessary to focus on something other than external conditions, such as market trends, and instead analyse your internal strategies, for example, your marketing, the quality of customer service, or the overall quality of your products.

When confronted by an intimidating problem, breaking it down into tiny, more tractable pieces is sometimes a helpful thing to do. This makes the problem not only less intimidating but also possible to solve, one segment at a time. By dealing with these small chunks in turn, you can steadily make your way towards an all-encompassing solution, rendering the whole activity less daunting and more feasible.

Creating many different possible solutions is essential during the problem-solving stage. Don't be content with the initial thought that arises, but spend some time thinking out of the box and weighing various alternatives. Consultation with other people may also yield new insights; don't shy away from consulting mentors, friends, or peers who can provide helpful input. Once you've settled on a solution, act promptly, but remain flexible—if your initial approach doesn't yield the desired results, be prepared to adapt and try again, as perseverance is essential in overcoming obstacles.

People usually encounter personal challenges that may stifle their growth and development. These challenges range from lack of motivation, general self-doubt, and extreme fear of failure. To overcome such challenges, it is crucial to set small and attainable goals that can be incrementally fulfilled. Being surrounded by optimistic and supportive people can also foster a motivating atmosphere. Moreover, the exercise of self-compassion and focusing on personal development over seeking perfection can also greatly increase one's mental resilience.

In business, some of the challenges that can face an organization include financial struggles, slow growth, and stiff competition. To effectively overcome these challenges, it is essential to critically analyse the current business model and be receptive to constructive criticism. Pivoting the business strategy, if need be, can open up new opportunities. In addition, the identification of cost-cutting areas, improving operational effectiveness, or accessing untapped markets can give a competitive advantage and drive sustainable development.

Relationship dynamics can also be very challenging, such as miscommunication, conflict, and trust issues. To solve these issues, practicing active listening is crucial, as it creates a better understanding between individuals. Being honest and open about one's feelings can lead to meaningful conversations, while compromise can resolve conflicts peacefully. Finally, emphasizing building trust and understanding is key in fostering healthy and long-term relationships so that individuals can better work through their interpersonal issues.

There was a time in my life when it felt like everything was crumbling. I had big dreams, but I faced a string of obstacles that seemed impossible to overcome—financial struggles, failed business ventures, and a persistent feeling of self-doubt. It felt like no matter how much progress I made, things would somehow manage to push me back even harder, and I would be left discouraged and doubting my direction.

Instead of giving up, I decided to change my attitude. I realized that every setback offered a chance for learning and growth. Through all this, I developed my time management skills, learned to be resilient, and how to keep my concentration even in the midst of challenges. With time, the setbacks that had seemed so daunting before turned into stepping stones that led me to my eventual success.

Looking back at those challenging times, I know that had it not been for those difficulties, I would not have come this far. Every failure was a lesson in disguise, which melded my character and strengthened my will. Now, I stand on the platform constructed from those very challenges, thankful for the journey that brought me to this point.

Accepting setbacks is a crucial part of any journey to success. The road to success is not always straight; it is typically lined with a series of hurdles and setbacks that may seem daunting at times. But the true test of success is the ability to get up after every fall. Rather than seeing setbacks as failures, take them as an integral part of your development. Every step back is a lesson that will push you forward, validating the fact that perseverance is the key to making sense of your own ambitions.

Building mental resilience is essential when faced with challenges. During times of adversity, you should tap into your inner reserves and look back at past successes. Recalling the obstacles you have overcome in the past can be a great motivator, reminding you that you have the ability to overcome present challenges. By building a mindset that incorporates resilience, you can turn challenges into chances for development, enabling you to come out of difficult circumstances even more powerful than ever.

It is critical to keep your sights on your grander aspirations when confronted with short-term adversities. A person can easily get derailed by immediate problems, but staying true to your vision will help you ride out the storms. Reflect on why you started this journey, and allow that fire to drive you. By focusing on the larger picture, you are able to ensure that temporary setbacks do not jeopardize your long-term goals so that you are able to remain true to your course and eventually attain the success you want.

Taking part in regular exercises to sharpen your problem-solving skills can prove to be highly valuable. Begin by spending a few minutes each day going over a particular challenge you faced and the strategy you employed to address it. Not only does this help foster a critical thinking mindset, but it also pushes you to proactively search for solutions instead of ruminating over the problems at hand. Through consistent practice, over time, this routine can strongly hone your problem-solving skills and increase your confidence in overcoming subsequent challenges.

Another good approach is to imagine your problems as stepping stones along the path of success. Draw a diagram or drawing with each stone representing a problem that you were able to overcome. This visualization is a strong reminder that every problem that you will encounter is not only a setback but a chance to learn and move forward. With this understanding of your challenges, you can adopt a more positive attitude and encourage yourself to accept new challenges as part of the process.

Also, negative thoughts that happen when faced with problems need to be addressed and turned around. Start by writing down your immediate pessimistic thoughts towards a scenario. After finding these thoughts, then spend time turning them around into positive, solution-based declarations. For example, rather than dwell on, "I couldn't possibly have passed this project," you can change it to, "This project has given me some lessons that can be used in future projects." This change in mindset not only reduces stress but also empowers you to focus on learning and improvement.

Most people tend to struggle with numerous issues, and this makes them come up with a chain of typical excuses that may hamper their development. For instance, when faced with a daunting task, one might think, "This is too hard." However, a more constructive perspective would be to acknowledge the difficulty while embracing the opportunity for personal development by saying, "This is challenging, but I'm learning and growing from it." Similarly, the belief that "I always fail" can be transformed into a more empowering mindset by recognizing that setbacks are merely stepping stones on the path to success, as one might say, "Failure is part of the process. Each setback brings me closer to success."

Yet another common excuse is this sense of being lost or in a muddle, usually phrased as, "I don't know what to do." Rather than yielding to this confusion, one has the option of taking a proactive stance with the words, "I'll take it one step at a time and ask for help if I need it." Another common sentiment, drawn together in the phrase, "Why does this always happen to me?" can be reconceptualized to promote resilience and a growth mindset. By seeing challenges as a chance for self-growth, one can say, "This is happening for me, not to me. It's an opportunity to grow." This change in attitude not only empowers but also motivates people to welcome their journeys with hope and resilience.

Life is naturally full of obstacles, but these obstacles do not have to hold you back. By changing your mindset and seeing challenges as opportunities for growth, you can tap into the power to turn setbacks into lessons that move you forward. Every challenge you face is a stepping stone, adding to your growth into a stronger, wiser, and more capable person.

When confronted with challenges, rather than avoiding them, go into them with an open mind and a learning spirit. Welcome the experience, learn the lessons it has to teach, and let it take you to greater heights. In doing so, not only do you ride through life's challenges, but you also come out stronger and better prepared to face life's next challenge, eventually attaining success far beyond your first expectations.

Reflection Questions for the Reader:

1. What's a recent problem I faced, and what did I learn from it?
2. How can I shift my mindset to see problems as opportunities?
3. What's one challenge I'm currently facing, and what's the first step I can take to solve it?

Chapter 10

Your network is your net worth

The role of relationships in our lives too often goes unsung, yet they are extremely important in building our experiences and opportunities. The saying, "It's not what you know, it's who you know," highlights that although skills and knowledge are crucial, the networks we build may have a critical impact on the path to achievement. The people around you—friends, mentors, colleagues, or professionals in your field—can be the portal to new opportunities, presenting advice, encouragement, and introductions that can take you further than you'd ever imagined.

In this chapter, we will explore the power of change that comes with nurturing and sustaining significant relationships. Through learning about the dynamics of your network, you are able to harness these relationships to better your personal and professional life. The reality is, the strength of your relationships can do a lot in terms of making you a more valuable person, and thus it is crucial that you take the time and effort to build a strong network that resonates with your dreams and ambitions.

The term "Your Network Is Your Net Worth" summarizes the concept that the people you network with can make a huge difference in your personal and professional success. Opportunities tend to come your way through the people you network with, in the form of job opportunities, business partnerships, or new ideas. A strong and diverse network can serve as a catalyst, opening many doors that would otherwise be shut, thus increasing your chances of growth and success.

Challenges are inevitable in life and business, and with a good network, you have a support system that can be critical at times of hardship. When confronted with challenges, members of your network can give you priceless advice, emotional support, and encouragement to guide you through tough moments. Not only is this sense of belongingness supportive in building resilience, but also it inspires a spirit of cooperation where you can share struggles and achieve triumphs together.

In addition to offering opportunities, your network can be a reservoir of learning and self-improvement. The interaction with individuals who have differing experiences and talent sets can improve your growth while avoiding pitfalls commonly encountered. With the sharing of knowledge and observations, you get a wider range of vision necessary for making prudent decisions and, in general, being more effective in personal as well as business life.

The importance of relationships in personal as well as professional life cannot be overemphasized. Success of numerous entrepreneurs is a direct result of networks they have established over years. These associations naturally give rise to successful joint ventures, collaborative strategic partnerships, and priceless mentorship, which all can boost the business ahead. By taking the initiative to work with others in their industry, individuals are able to access an enormous amount of information and resources that may otherwise be unavailable to them, reinforcing the need for developing and fostering a strong professional network.

At a personal level, the company you keep determines your development and growth. Surrounding yourself with ambitious and motivational people can inspire you to excel and go beyond your capabilities. The fact that you are the average of the five people you spend most of your time with is a strong reminder to select your friends wisely. By building friendships with people who confront and inspire you, you allow yourself an atmosphere that promotes improvement and achievement as an individual.

Life is usually full of surprises, and at times, a casual conversation or an accidental meeting can lead to great opportunities. The more people you meet, the higher the chances of finding a chance that will alter your life. Every new connection has the potential to bring unforeseen success, either through collaborative ideas, joint projects, or referrals to other powerful people. Embracing the uncertainty of networking can result in a treasure of opportunities that add value to both your professional and personal life.

Building a strong network starts with sincerity. People can quickly tell when an individual is insincere or is only looking out for his or her interests. To build real relationships, start by being honest and open in your interactions. Network with a spirit of generosity, hoping to give value to others without necessarily expecting an immediate return. This sincerity provides the foundation for trust and respect, and these are foundational elements for long-term connections.

Participating in networking sessions is another viable approach to building your professional network. Whether you prefer attending industry meetups, seminars, or city events, such events provide unique opportunities to associate with people with similar interests and possible partners. By getting into these scenes, not only are you exposed to the latest developments and techniques but also build a platform to spark conversations that might result in effective collaborations. The secret is being open and welcoming, maximizing the potential of every encounter.

You can really boost your networking potential by tapping into social networking sites. LinkedIn, Twitter, and Instagram are great places to post your ideas, network with colleagues, and connect with the leaders in your field. Don't be afraid to go after the people you respect; a friendly hello can lead to some very interesting doors. And don't forget to follow up on these connections—check in with your contacts, post of interest to them, and congratulate them when they achieve something. By continually providing encouragement and support, you establish yourself in your network and create a community of cooperation and development.

The importance of having mentors and role models in your life cannot be emphasized enough. Mentors are people who have walked similar roads and can offer priceless advice based on their own experiences. They act as guides, assisting you in overcoming obstacles and steering clear of pitfalls that can sidetrack your progress. Through the sharing of their knowledge and lessons acquired, mentors can light the way ahead, making your journey easier and better informed.

When looking for the appropriate mentor, it's important to find someone who shares your values and whose success is indicative of the success you'd like to achieve. This commonality is important, as it allows for relevant and useful guidance in your specific circumstances. Don't be afraid to go to potential mentors; successful people are often willing to impart their knowledge to those who show a sincere dedication to personal and professional development. Asking for advice can lead to doors opening to significant relationships that support your growth.

Apart from looking for direct mentorship, you can also learn from role models, even if they are not directly available. Through learning about the lives of people you look up to, either through their written materials, interviews, or public appearances, you can learn valuable lessons and strategies that can guide your own path. Watching them succeed and fail helps you develop a deeper appreciation for what it takes to get what you want, in the end allowing you to create your own destiny with confidence and clarity.

The value of keeping company with positive people cannot be underscored enough. The people you surround yourself with will determine how you think and how high you can aspire. When you surround yourself with people who exude optimism and support, they are likely to inspire you to go after your dreams. On the other hand, when your friends and acquaintances are filled with negativity and pessimism, it can suffocate your development and passion. Hence, it is important to make a deliberate choice of friends and social contacts who push you to be your best and who promote your goals. It is an important skill for personal growth to know when it is time to cut ties with harmful relationships. Not all relationships are good, and some can even hold you back. If you notice that there are people who regularly drain your self-confidence, dismiss your aspirations, or stir up unnecessary drama, then it might be time to rethink their position in your life. Taking care of yourself requires making tough decisions, such as keeping your distance from those who are not helping to move your life in a positive direction.

Accepting a multigenerational network can vastly improve your personal and professional development. Restricting your network to those with your background or perspective can cause you to stagnate. By talking with people from different backgrounds, industries, and experiences, you expose yourself to volumes of fresh ideas and insights. This diversity not only broadens your knowledge of the world, but it also breeds creativity and innovation, leading you ultimately to greater success.

The tale of Steve Jobs and Steve Wozniak is an inspiring example of the strength of networking. Their meeting was a result of a common friend, which eventually contributed to the development of Apple Inc., a business that would revolutionize the technological world. The world could have been denied with innovative products like the iPhone and MacBook if they had not had that first point of contact. This case shows how one introduction can trigger a series of creativity and entrepreneurship, pointing to the value of relationship building and maintenance in the technology sector.

Oprah Winfrey's path to media mogul status is inextricably linked with her friendship with Maya Angelou. Oprah frequently discusses how Angelou was both a mentor and a close friend who helped her navigate life and career challenges. This relationship not only impacted Oprah's world view but also had a considerable influence on the direction of her career. The effect of their relationship highlights the deep influence that mentorship can have and how helpful relationships can help to develop people and encourage them to be their best.

LinkedIn co-founder Reid Hoffman is the epitome of how networking can form the basis of a lucrative career. His capacity to establish relationships has played a critical role in his business ventures, from founding LinkedIn to investing in some of the world's most high-profile companies, including PayPal and Airbnb. Hoffman's testament is a strong reminder that in business, success tends to rest on the bonds one develops. By drawing on his connections, he not only progressed in his own career but has been instrumental in the success of many startups, illustrating the potential to transform lives through strategic networking.

In order to truly cultivate and develop your professional network, it is important that you keep in touch with your contacts on a regular basis. Instead of simply building relationships and then disappearing from view, establish a routine of staying in touch every now and again. Sending a quick hello or passing on an article or piece of information that you think they would be interested in reading will keep communication lines open and show that you respect the connection.

Being there for your contacts in both their successes and failures is important to building a strong network. Share in their successes with sincere excitement, but also provide support in times of need. This mutual relationship forms a basis of trust and dependability, furthering the notion that a strong network is built on the exchange of help and knowledge.

Organizing events or meetups is also a great means of cementing your position within your network. Whether you decide on a casual coffee catch-up or something more formal, making the effort to bring others together not only serves to enhance existing relationships but also places you in the centre as a main connector within your group. Also, showing appreciation in small ways, like thank-you cards, can really strengthen your connections, creating a lasting impact and further strengthening bonds.

If you find yourself to be an introvert, do not worry about networking at all. The key to networking is not being the loudest person in the room, but instead building significant, intimate connections with people. Don't try to talk to everyone in the room, but instead work on building individual connections that open doors to deeper conversations. This method enables you to present your strengths and establish an easy-to-be-with atmosphere where honest talks can grow.

The fear of rejection is a major obstacle when it comes to networking, but it's also important to remember that not all outreach will result in a positive response. Keep in mind that rejection is an inherent part of the networking process, and it should not stop you from reaching out to others. Every encounter is a chance to learn and develop, and by continuing your efforts, you will sooner or later come across the appropriate connections that will appeal to your aspirations and ambitions.

It's natural to feel that you have very little to offer in networking situations, but it's essential to keep in mind that every individual has something different to offer. If you offer a fresh view, helpful resources, or merely a desire to assist, your input is important. Be yourself and see the value in what you have to offer in creating relationships. Through placing value on the contributions you offer, you may establish relationships which are enriching and mutually useful.

Developing and expanding your professional network is a key part of career growth. One good exercise is to identify five people in your field whom you strongly admire. Sit down and learn about their histories, successes, and what they are working on now. After you have a good sense of what they do, write a personal note to contact them. This is an approach that not only shows your actual interest but also provides the avenue for deep connections that can help advance your career.

Another strong tactic is to make a promise to yourself to attend a minimum of one networking event per month, either virtual or in-person. The importance here is that you focus more on the depth of your conversations than the frequency of events that you attend. Getting deeply connected with even one individual can give rise to big opportunities and collaborations. By establishing this goal, you establish a regular rhythm of networking that can assist you in remaining connected and updated about your industry.

In addition, you may want to start a network gratitude journal. Each week, write down three people you thank and why you're thankful. Not only will this practice cement your relationships but remind you to regularly cultivate those ties. As an exercise, take the initiative to contact a person every week who you do not know, whether it is a mutual friend, professional, or someone you have always admired but never approached. These interactions can create surprising opportunities and make your career life more fulfilling.

In short, the relationships you build over your lifetime are among your most valuable assets. Those relationships can lead you down new paths, unlock potential doors, and speed you on your way to achieving your goals in ways that you may never have dreamed of. It's vital to recognize that networking is not about self-serving self-interest; it's about the mutual exchange of support, encouragement, and growth.

Start to grow your network today by being you and providing value to others. Be around people who inspire and support you, for their impact can be profound. With a proper support group, the sky is the limit to what you can achieve, and you'll see that as a group, you can attain levels previously impossible to reach.

Reflection Questions for the Reader:

1. Who are the top five people in my current network that inspire me?
2. How can I add value to the people in my network today?
3. What steps can I take to expand my network and connect with new people?

Chapter 11

Growth comes from discomfort

Life offers a vast array of possibilities, but many people tend to miss out on them because they are afraid to step outside their comfort zones. Whether it's starting something new, learning a new skill, or even changing daily routines, the idea of embracing the unknown can be intimidating. But the truth is, real personal growth happens when you challenge your limits and face your fears directly.

In this chapter, we're going to explore why it's necessary to step outside your comfort zone, discuss the ways that fear can get in the way of progress, and provide actionable techniques to enable you to embrace new experiences into your life. As a reminder, every expert had to begin from a place of being a novice; without stepping out for the first time, you'll never know the extent of what you're capable of. Venturing into the unknown can create spectacular growth and transformation.

Adopting new experiences is important for self-growth and knowing oneself on a deeper level. Every time you step into the unknown, you discover aspects of your personality that could have gone unnoticed. This process of discovery can unveil hidden talents and interests, enabling you to connect with your true self in ways you never expected. The process of trying new things not only enhances your self-awareness but also enriches your life with diverse experiences that contribute to your overall growth.

Venturing out of your comfort zone is an incredibly effective tool for developing self-confidence. As you face new challenges, you slowly discover your ability to overcome what previously appeared to be insurmountable. This developing strength gives you a sense of empowerment, prompting you to push further boundaries in the future. With each success, your confidence grows, reinforcing the notion that you are capable of achieving great things, creating a positive feedback cycle that promotes ongoing exploration.

Participating in new things unlocks a whole universe of opportunity that can make a huge difference in the trajectory of your life. These new experiences tend to bring about spontaneous meetings with people who can teach or motivate you, and learning about interests that fuel your passion. Moreover, doing something new can reveal hidden career opportunities or interests that resonate with you, ultimately making your life richer. Through this freedom from routine, you not only energize your daily life but also nurture a mind that is open to the countless opportunities that life can present.

The fear of venturing into new experiences is usually born out of an underlying fear of failure. Most people are reluctant to venture out of their comfort zones for fear of failing. But it is important to note that failure is not the opposite of success; instead, it is a necessary part of the learning process. Every setback presents valuable lessons which can bring you closer to realizing your goals and turn what first appears as failure into a stepping stone for accomplishment.

Another important obstacle to the adoption of new possibilities is the fear of judgments from others. Such a fear can be so pervasive that it suppresses imagination and discovery. However, it's important to know that most people are engrossed in their own lives and are not going to scrutinize your actions as much as you worry about. By moving your attention from the opinions of others to your own satisfaction, you can free yourself from the restrictions of other people's views and follow what actually speaks to you.

The unease of the unknown is a universal human condition, which most often results in reluctance to venture into the new. Although it is absolutely normal to be apprehensive about something new, one should welcome this uncertainty as a fertile soil for self-development. The more you face the unknown, the better you become at dealing with it, eventually building resilience and adaptability. Also, striving for perfection can be a hindrance to progress; knowing that perfection is an ideal that cannot be reached enables you to see the worth in beginning, even if it is imperfectly.

Venturing outside of the comfortable borders of your comfort zone can bring about the development of dormant qualities that you might not have known you had. People frequently discover their greatest talents only after they're willing to make a leap of faith and venture into the unknown. By pushing yourself and taking calculated risks, you unlock the potential for self-discovery and personal growth, revealing in yourself strengths once hidden beneath the surface.

Trying new things widens your vision and exposes you to a vibrant weave of ideas, cultures, and worldviews. Through exposure, you gain an appreciation of open-mindedness, embracing diversity and the ability to accommodate diverse situations with less difficulty. While you venture into new places, you gain a better insight into the world, which can promote better interpersonal relationships and richer life experiences.

Taking on challenges is a great way to become resilient, since every challenge that you overcome provides you with the skills necessary to deal with problems in the future. The more you challenge your comfort zone, the better you will become at dealing with life's natural ebbs and flows. Also, these experiences have the ability to spark creativity within you, and you'll start thinking creatively, looking at issues from different perspectives, and developing innovative solutions that you wouldn't have even thought of previously.

J.K. Rowling's life is a tribute to determination and perseverance. Before she became a towering success as a writer, she faced an onslaught of rejections from multiple publishing companies. Instead of being deterred by this, Rowling refused to give up, and her steadfast confidence in her work eventually gave rise to the Harry Potter series that captured the imaginations of millions and made her a literary phenomenon across the world.

Elon Musk is the epitome of innovation and risk-taking in the contemporary era. Having moved from his initial business ventures with PayPal, he took bold steps into electric cars with Tesla and space travel with SpaceX. Musk's willingness to venture into the unknown and question the status quo has not only taken his own career to new heights but has also initiated dramatic developments in several sectors, inspiring millions of others to think out of the box.

The life of Colonel Sanders is an inspirational example of how one's age should never be an obstacle to realizing one's ambitions. Having received more than a thousand rejections, he finally opened up KFC when he was 65 years old, establishing that it is never too early or too late to start something new. His life is indicative of the virtues of perseverance and the notion that success is at any point of life, in order to incite others into taking great steps towards their ambition despite their lives.

Start your journey of discovery by taking small, achievable steps. There is no need to revolutionize your life overnight; rather, begin with small changes that can create large results in the long run. Try a new recipe that interests you, take a different route during your daily drive, or read a book that falls outside of your usual reading habits. These tiny steps can spark a spirit of adventure and introduce your mind to the possibilities of new experiences without overwhelming you.

Challenge yourself by making personal goals that push you outside of your comfort zone. Think about committing to learning a new skill every month or going out of your way to meet new people at social events. These personal challenges not only help you grow as a person but also build your confidence as you push through new experiences. Taking on these challenges can change your outlook, and the world will seem more alive and full of promise.

Fostering a growth mindset is key to accepting new experiences. This allows you to recognize challenges as chances to grow instead of threats to be stayed away from. Having faith in your ability to learn and improve by effort, you can tackle new endeavours with excitement and fortitude. Moreover, it is necessary to have positive self-talk about your efforts irrespective of success or failure. Recognize the bravery involved in attempting something new, for every attempt, successful or not, is a part of your own journey and development. Being around positive people who support your experimentation can also increase your readiness to accept change and risk.

Acquiring Failure as a Learning Experience: Every failure offers an individual opportunity for expansion. Rather than perceiving failure as an end point, look at it as a useful lesson waiting to be discovered. By questioning yourself about what you can learn from every experience, you can turn disappointments into stepping stones towards success. This attitude change not only builds resilience but also provides you with the insight necessary to deal with such problems better in the future.

The Value of Quick Experimentation: Success is sometimes paved with failures, and the earlier you accept this fact, the faster you will mature. Venturing into new activities and embracing failure as a possibility enables you to speed up your learning curve. Through a mindset that looks at fast iterations and early failure as important, you can learn critical feedback that guides you in your next steps, leading to better-informed decisions and novel solutions.

The Importance of Perseverance: Succeeding at your goals is rarely an easy journey; more often than not, it involves persistence in the face of challenge. Most successful people have had to overcome setbacks and failures on their paths, but what distinguishes them is their refusal to give up. By developing a spirit of perseverance, you not only develop character but also raise your chances of ultimate success. Keep in mind, each obstacle that you overcome will contribute to your resilience and will prepare you for the victories ahead.

One effective way to broaden your horizons is to embark on a "30-Day New Thing" challenge. This involves dedicating yourself to experiencing something novel each day for an entire month. The activities can range from sampling a different cuisine to initiating a conversation with someone you've never met, or even picking up a new hobby. Not only does this challenge push you out of your comfort zone, but it also presents a universe of opportunities that you might not have otherwise thought of.

Another intense exercise is the creation of a "Fear List." First, write down every activity or experience that frightens you. After you have your list, put the fears in order from least intimidating to most overwhelming. This systematic process enables you to face your fears step by step, addressing them individually. By facing these fears head-on, you'll likely discover that many of them are not as frightening as they initially seemed, leading to personal growth and increased confidence.

Having a "New Experiences" journal is another revolutionary practice. Write down in the journal each new venture that you take, your thoughts on it, and how you felt during the experience. As the months go by, you'll be able to review and recognize how far you have come, not only the amount of diverse experiences you've gained but also how much you have grown emotionally in the process. Also, for one week, make a conscious effort to be more of a "yes" person. By saying "yes" to those opportunities that you would normally turn down, you might find yourself presented with surprising and rewarding situations that add depth to your life in ways you never expected.

To take the leap and step into the unknown can dramatically affect the lives of those you surround yourself with. By initiating new experiences for yourself, you challenge yourself and inspire others to push beyond their own boundaries. Your openness to change can awaken a spark within friends, loved ones, and co-workers and inspire them to seek out their own adventures and changes. This ripple effect has the potential to create a culture of people who are more accepting of expansion and discovery, and where innovation and creativity can flourish.

Taking the leap out of your comfortable bubble can mean a life filled with excitement and fulfilment. With every new experience you take on, you enrich yourself and learn to connect more profoundly with other people and find a new sense of purpose. As you get involved in a variety of activities and points of view, you gain a greater knowledge of the world, and this can bring about a higher level of happiness and contentment. The excitement of doing something different can energize your daily life, making life more exciting and worthwhile.

As you keep pushing yourself to experiment and try new things, you will find your way of thinking completely changing. Tasks that seemed frightening at first will become more comfortable, and things that initially intimidated you will become second nature. This process not only boosts your confidence but also develops your resilience, which prepares you for confronting challenges ahead with a good attitude. With time, you will discover that your openness to the unknown not only enhances your own existence but also enables you to inspire others to set out on their own path of discovery.

To summarize, venturing out of your comfort zone is where life actually starts. Undertaking new experiences is more than just pursuing success; it is about embracing the fullness of life. In embracing uncertainty, you open a world full of possibilities. Though the path might be filled with setbacks and failures, every problem you encounter leads to your growth, making you stronger, wiser, and ultimately happier with your life.

Thus, go ahead and take that first step into the unknown. Whether it is starting a new business, learning a new ability, or just venturing down a new road, remember that self-improvement thrives in the unknown. Life is a great adventure to be lived—make sure you take each moment and live it to its maximum capacity.

Reflection Questions for the Reader:

1. What's one new thing I've been afraid to try, and what's holding me back?
2. How can I reframe my fear of failure into an opportunity for growth?
3. What small step can I take today to step out of my comfort zone?

Chapter 12

Success is a journey, not a destination—have commas, but no full stops

The idea of success is commonly misunderstood as a one-time endpoint, a destination where one can finally rest and Savor the fruits of his labour. Nonetheless, the truth is that success is more like a continuous journey of experiences instead of a conclusive end. It evolves as a series of moments that lead to development, continuous learning, and alteration. Reaching a goal does not mean the end, but it leads to new challenges and opportunities that make our lives even richer.

In this chapter, we will explore the concept that success is a long-term process, where the focus will be on appreciating the journey rather than the goal. Knowing that success is not just a place to be reached but a way of life to be lived can have a dramatic effect on us. We will cover methods for keeping momentum and motivation, no matter where you are at on your journey. By understanding that success is a changing and dynamic experience, you can develop a mindset that feeds on growth and resilience.

The "Ultimate Achievement" Concept is Deceptive: Success is a concept that means many different things to different people. To some, it is synonymous with financial success or popular acclaim, to others it might be about personal satisfactions, happiness, or fostering meaningful relationships. Irrespective of the definition of success, it is fundamental to realize that it is not a one-time achievement but one of continuous processes involving a series of successes and worthwhile learning experiences.

Achievements Are Not the End of the Road: Reaching a specific milestone may sometimes bring a false impression of accomplishment, and as a result, people may feel that they have already attained the peak of their potential. But life is a process that never ends, and self-development ought to be a persistent effort. Most end up in a posture of complacency upon reaching the milestone, learning only that sustainable growth is a never-ending challenge that calls for relentless effort and flexibility.

The Dangers of Treating Success as an End Point: When success is seen as an end point, it can create a perilous stagnation. This creates complacency, which can lead to boredom, dissatisfaction, and eventually, a loss of motivation. In order to really thrive, it is essential to be open to change and dedicated to individual growth, so that the quest for success is an ongoing journey and not a destination to be attained.

Looking at success as a series of commas instead of periods can shift the way we view our successes. Every achievement we make is a temporary halt in our never-ending story, and we can take time to appreciate our efforts and rejoice over our accomplishments. Be it the finishing of a degree, acquiring a new job, or launching an enterprise, these are not end points but stepping stones that take us to newer things and experiences that await us.

It's essential to prioritize progress over perfection in the pursuit of success. It's critical to understand that the road to success is seldom a linear path; rather, it is dotted with twists, turns, and small steps. Every little success is part of the big picture, and every effort matters, reminding us that growth often occurs through trial and error instead of getting perfect results from the beginning.

Visualizing life as a vibrant tapestry of tales instead of one, fixed sentence permits a more dynamic comprehension of our lives. Every achievement adds depth and richness to our own story, making our journey richer. The beauty of life is in its unfolding pages, where every success pushes us forward, urging us to keep writing our tale and accepting the growth that comes with every new venture.

The importance of ongoing education cannot be overemphasized. The people who enjoy tremendous success typically have the learning spirit, continually seeking new wisdom, abilities, and experiences to enrich their existence. This restlessness for knowing serves as the driving force in personal and career growth, impelling them towards unexplored frontiers and broadening the horizons of their existence.

In an ever-changing world, the power of adaptation is key to achieving success. Whether it's with regards to technology advancements, changes in the corporate world, or self-improvement, being open to learning provides one with the mechanisms needed to navigate such changes. The power of embracing new experiences and knowledge makes one relevant and strong in the midst of changing circumstances.

Having a growth mindset is necessary for anyone who wishes to succeed in a constantly evolving world. This mindset encourages the idea that one can always get better through hard work and study. By seeing obstacles as opportunities for growth instead of roadblocks, people can develop resilience and an active attitude towards their lives and careers.

To reach success is realized through different levels, each with a unique effect on our entire well-being. Individual success is the accomplishment of factors like cultivating your health, developing relationships with depth, and embracing joy within your daily routine. These aspects are essential and need to be equated on par with workplace success, since they are what establish a gratifying life.

On the professional side, success is typically characterized by important milestones such as being given promotions, starting a new business, or achieving certain financial milestones. Although these successes are important and can bring about a feeling of fulfilment, they are merely a part of the larger picture of success. It is crucial to understand that professional growth must support, and not dominate, personal development and happiness.

Additionally, real success is not just about material wealth and professional achievements; it also involves emotional and spiritual satisfactions. Finding inner peace, building emotional resilience, and finding a fulfilling purpose in life are all essential elements of a balanced success story. Finding the right balance between these different aspects is crucial for a rich and fulfilling life experience.

The story of ongoing success is effectively described by the life of Steve Jobs. Having co-founded Apple, he was dealt a major blow when he was expelled from the same company he had founded. Instead of giving in to failure, Jobs directed his imagination towards starting up Pixar, which revolutionized the animation sector. His return to Apple later in his life proved to be the turning point, as he led the charge for innovations that would revolutionize technology and consumer electronics. Jobs' path is a demonstration of perseverance, highlighting that failures can be stepping stones and not dead ends.

Serena Williams is the epitome of dogged determination, moving beyond her successful tennis career to pursue a variety of pursuits. With an impressive tally of championships to her name, she has branched out into the worlds of business, fashion, and charity, proving that her determination is far from limited to the tennis court. Williams has never shied away from new opportunities and challenges, demonstrating that real success is not all about achievement but also about ongoing development and exploration in new areas. Her growth as a multidimensional individual inspires others to pursue their passions without boundaries.

Nelson Mandela's life is a deep reflection of purpose and perseverance. Surviving 27 years in prison, he came out not as a victim but as a symbol of hope and reconciliation for South Africa. Mandela's leadership during the post-apartheid period played a key role in uniting and healing a nation that was divided. His legacy is transnational, having become a symbol of peace, justice, and the strength of perseverance that endured for centuries to come. The story of Mandela teaches us that lasting impact is not about what is endured but by what kind of change one can create in the world.

Succeeding is an amazing achievement, but there is a need to keep the momentum going by establishing new goals. After you have attained a specific goal, think about what is next. This may mean seeking additional personal growth or career advancement. By constantly pushing yourself with new targets, you not only sustain your motivation but also develop a growth and discovery mindset. Every new achievement is a stepping stone, leading you to even higher achievements.

While it's important to take a moment to reflect on and celebrate your achievements, it's equally crucial to recognize that these victories are part of a larger journey. Acknowledging your successes can provide a sense of fulfilments and motivation, but they should not be seen as the end of the road. Instead, view them as milestones that pave the way for future endeavours. This balance of looking back and looking ahead guarantees that you stay active and interested in what's next.

Furthermore, actual success is sometimes gauged not only by individual accomplishments but also by how you affect others. Performing good deeds, mentoring newcomers, or giving back to your community can make your own journey more rewarding and give you a sense of direction. Finally, staying humble is essential; regardless of how far you've progressed, there is always something new to learn and discover. Adopting this attitude keeps you on your feet and ready to keep on growing, making your journey rich and rewarding.

Embracing failures as part of your process is crucial for growth. Instead of seeing failure as an absolute conclusion, see it as a temporary halt in your story. Every failure is a lesson, and it Molds your character and directs you towards your dreams. By embracing these failures, you learn things that drive you forward, turning failures into stepping stones towards success.

The defining characteristic of genuine resilience is your ability to bounce back from adversity. It is this same quality that separates those who succeed in their dreams from those who fail and give up on their endeavours. Success is not gauged by the absence of failures but by the will to get up after every fall. Building resilience is about recognizing your setbacks but having the strength to keep pushing forward towards your aspirations, regardless of how many times you fall in the process.

Along the way, adversity will strike and challenge your commitment and determination. But it's also important to recall that so long as you're willing to continue, the journey never truly ends. With each obstacle is the chance to learn and to grow, serving as a reminder that the close of one door is the start of another. By staying focused on forward motion and keeping your eyes on progress, you can use each failure as a springboard for success.

Creating a Vision Beyond Individual Goals: Although specific goals are essential for advancement, creating a vision of a broader scope can inspire your passion and motivation in the long term. Rather than concentrating solely on individual successes, invest your time in imagining the life you want to establish. This overall vision will not just direct your actions but also give you a sense of purpose deeper than mere motivation.

Recording Your Progress: Keeping a record of your achievements can be an excellent motivator. Keeping a journal or list of your successes can help you see visually how far you've come and think about the progress you've made. This habit not only reaffirms your dedication but also reminds you of your strength and ability, so you're motivated to keep going even when things get tough.

Creating a Support Network: Your network of relationships is an essential part of establishing your mindset and goals. Getting around people with a growth perspective can motivate you to excel more than ever. Find a supportive group that pressures you, gives you credit where it is due, and strives to learn throughout life, since such a surrounding network can contribute immensely to the growth of the individual and in professional life as well.

In conclusion, it's crucial to appreciate that your path is a never-ending story and not a destination. Success is a journey to be seen as a constant progression, full of surprise twists and new beginnings. Every milestone you achieve is a break in your story, a time to think and not a conclusion. The most fulfilling lives are those filled with purpose, passion, and the knowledge that personal development is a lifelong process.

As you forge on your own path, be sure to celebrate your successes, learn from your failures, and hold onto your hope for the future. The most thrilling moments of life are the ones that take place when you accept that there are always fresh pages to be written. Leave your pen poised and your heart receptive, because the journey of writing your story is only just beginning.

Reflection Questions for the Reader:

1. What does success mean to me beyond just achieving goals?
2. How can I continue growing even after reaching my current goals?
3. What new challenges or opportunities can I embrace in the next phase of my journey?